The Heart Centered JOURNEY

SHA'LEDA MIRRA

WWW.13THANDJOAN.COM

2019 by Sha'Leda Mirra

Published by 13th & Joan

All rights reserved. No part of this publication may be reproduced, distributed, or transmitted in any form or by any means, including photocopying, recording, or other electronic or mechanical methods, without the prior written permission of the publisher, except in the case of brief quotations embodied in critical reviews and certain other noncommercial uses permitted by copyright law. For permission requests, write to the publisher, addressed "Attention: Permissions Coordinator," at the address below.

13th & Joan
500 N. Michigan Avenue, Suite #600
Chicago, IL 60611
WWW.13THANDJOAN.COM

Ordering Information:
13th & Joan books may be purchased for educational, business or sales promotional use. For information, please email the Sales Department at sales@13thandjoan.com.

Printed in the United States of America

Publisher's Cataloging-in-Publication data has been applied for.

First Edition Printed, March 2019
Library of Congress Cataloging-in-Publication Data has been applied for.

First Edition
10 9 8 7 6 5 4 3 2 1

This my first literary work is dedicated to my father, the late Dale Roy Ellis.

THOUGH OUR TIME on earth was short lived, it was you who planted within me the seeds of limitless possibility. Even in the present moment, your voice resonates in my spirit, repeating the sacred chant that imbued vibrancy into my soul. A wise soul you were, embodying external struggles which illuminated the warrior on the inside of you. It was you who modeled the essence of neglecting the outer noise so that precision can be devoted to the inner voice within me. It was you who taught me that no matter what anyone else said, I was brave, bold, beautiful, intelligent, and able to be anything I wanted to be. You taught me that nothing was off limits as long as it was in God's will for my life. You pushed me to my limits! Now I realize that those were not limits at all, just boundaries of nothingness that I built within my mind that caused me to stop when there was no stop sign. So dad, I dedicate this book to you. The journey of becoming has not been easy, but every moment has been divine! I miss your voice and I look forward to dancing with you on the clouds that are higher than the sun, with the Son, in eternity.

Preface:
A LETTER TO THE INNER ME

Writing ... I cannot be, until my obedience sets me free. Writing ... I wrestle with you-like Jacob wrestled with the angel. It is with great fear and distress that I pen the issues of life, and the deepest schisms of my heart; yet I know that even though the sinew of my heart will be exposed, I will walk away with a great blessing.

Why? Because obedience is better than sacrifice.

I desire a release from the bondage of secrecy that has, for so long, kept me silent. So, beginning today, I repossess the courage to purge my soul through the power of my pen.

Writing, the cursed honor, has always been like music to my soul; I can hear the melody in my mind, yet, still.

Writing arrests my conscious mind, evokes a piercing pain that overwhelms my senses, and floods my fingertips with words that flow forth like a river.

The release of words from my subconscious is as painful as childbirth, but as liberating as soaring through the air on the shoulders of an eagle-it's like breathing air after being underwater.

Writing is captivating as it seizes the internal functioning of my entire being. Writing forces me to face my own authenticity, calling into question the very essence of who I am and who I am not.

Writing demands truth, because once it is written, it can never be erased.

It is the truth that sets you free, and the truth in these words march through me and onto the paper in front of me. Until each word is discharged from my being, escapes the confines of my heart, and emits its intent within the words that I write, I will write still, until these words meet the sound of your voice; an accompaniment of sound. I shall be free; I choose to release the inner me.

So here's to freedom ~ God told me to write.

In obedience, I write, so that my soul may be set free.

So that you may join me on this journey, a journey of the heart, while we both transform, predestination, manifestation, purpose fulfilled, obedience seen.

This is dedicated to you Lord, the audible voice of motivation in my ear, that triggers an intense yearning to be free.

Acknowledgments

I would like to extend gratitude to my husband and best friend, Christopher Mirra. I thank you for believing in me and not letting me quit when frustration and catastrophizing thoughts plagued my mind. When I was distracted, your kind and gentle redirection helped me focus on what was important to me, which was writing. There were so many times I wanted to give up, feeling buried by the cares of life. However, for every hole I dug to hide, you uncovered me. For every time I tried to hide, you found me. For every tear I shed, you made me laugh. Your unconditional love made all the difference. This book would not be, if it were not for your constant love and encouragement. I am thankful to God and His infinite wisdom that He chose to create you, and that He saved and preserved such a gift, for me!

Epigraph

Life is a Journey, a journey of the heart. In order to find yourself, you must search the deepest parts of you and while you are searching, not only will you find yourself … you will find someone greater, someone wiser, someone stronger … someone divine. You will find that the Spirit of the living God lives on the inside of you. Once you find God, the two of you become a dynamic duo as you navigate the labyrinth of life. Finding God will give you the courage to repossess the pen that authors the story of your life. You are the author, God is the narrator, now prepare for the journey toward your destiny. Be what God created you to be … a masterpiece created by divine hands in a divine image.

-Sha'Leda Mirra

The Symptom
OF BEING YOU:

There is a symptom, that each of us possesses.

A symptom that we see each time we look in the mirror.

A symptom that we feel each time we inhale … and exhale.

And, even when we pretend, the mask that was so carefully designed is intricately molded to the very shape of you because, let's not forget, its origin and the grand design with a goal to hide, finds its foundation and purpose … in you.

That symptom never dissipates it's ever present.

It's like skin … no matter how many tattoos, how much you try to bleach it, change it, estrange from it, it never goes away. It only scars; which adds, now, another chapter to the story, and another feature of the symptom of you!

This symptom, if left unchecked, creates a condition and an environment that you will never escape.

You metastasize.

Feeling trapped, with no one to relate … Within you is your only debate.

And, if you do not conform to the demands of you, the symptom breeds a form of self-hate.

Which motivates you to self mutilate based on your preferred method of choice in an attempt to imitate someone or something that, in the end, possesses the same symptoms as you.

The symptom of you, passed down through an entire generation from the garden.

A defect that we did not have upon conception when in the mind of God, yet, once birthed into this world, it attacks and plagues .

Sin the ever present instigator, fraudulent motivator, and the ticking time bomb detonator.

Causing one to die slowly.

The urge of you becomes so strong that you begin to look for everything you can to satiate the need that this symptom impresses upon your DNA.

It heightens your senses, triggering a loss of control.

Your psyche becomes obsessed with and overwhelmed by the desires.

And, consciously you find yourself overstimulated by … YOU.

Why is being YOU a symptom?

Because "you," is symbolic of anonymity. The symptom of you triggers a perception of self separate from the Grand Designer and Originator of Life … God.

You is a symptom because there is no awareness of US. There is no consultation in decision making with US. There is no consideration for how our decisions will impact US.

You encompasses a level of singularity, solidarity, and independence apart from God that asserts, "I am like God," and, "I am capable of making the choice between good and evil."

Being you asserts a self-sufficiency that finds its origin, its supply, and its ending from within.

You have a perceptual view that seeks exhalation, affirmation, glorification, omnipotence, if you will, preeminence.

Life is spent fiending and chasing after the lusts of you.

Know that the definition of a fiend is Satan, the devil; and when sin permeates your life, you become a fiend of you … the flesh.

This is why Romans 7:18-20[1] asserts, as penned by the apostle Paul, "For I know that nothing good dwells in me, that is, in my flesh. For I have the desire to do what is right, but not the ability to carry it out. For I do not do the good I want, but the evil I do not want is what I keep doing. Now if I do what I do not want, it is no longer I who do it, but sin that dwells within me."

You see, apart from the union of humanity with God, the indwelling of the Holy Spirit, there is never a transition from you.

Jeremiah 17:9[2] states that the heart is deceitful above all things and desperately sick. Who can understand it?

Out of the heart, flows the issues of life. The heart of YOU is the seat of soul and character. It is the essence and core of the persona, beliefs, and behaviors. You the symptom of you becomes, as so defined by Webster[3], a physical or mental feature indicative of disease; a sign of the existence of something undesirable.

An indication.

A mark.

A mutation of life, because the purpose for which you were created, and the justification that lies embedded in your DNA,morphs into something unnatural, anomalous, bizarre, eccentric.

True evolution into the pre-destined purpose and the supernatural identity that envelopes your soul, can only be when *you* become *us*, and are no longer identified as independent, but interdependent.

It is at the recognition of WE, God and I, the God that takes up residence in me, that is my source of strength, purpose, providence.

As I regurgitate all that life has taught me about the beauty of individuality and uniqueness, I, now, fully embrace that my only individuality and uniqueness lies in you; and that makes me the rarest of all that God created.

Union with God, makes me authentic.

Union with God, makes me truly beautiful.

The goal is transformation and transcendence from you, to transformation into His image with ever increasing glory, which comes from the Lord, who is the Spirit.

You is a symptom.

Us is divine.

In this natural world, we are taught to conform instead of transform. While diversity and uniqueness seeps from our DNA, we are taught that it is foreign to be different; we are taught that we should strive to be someone else, instead of our greatest self. We are forced to select a role model in the form of a person; and to create a replica instead of an authentic masterpiece. Societal norms from unqualified opinions have precipitated a lawless assault on individuality. Whispered lies come in every form, perpetuating the belief that acceptance comes in the form of conformity, and conformity only. If we fail to understand that we are to refuse to conform to this world, but instead, we are to be transformed by the renewing of our minds, we will lose ourselves and become a poor duplicate of a duplicate, a photocopy of a photocopy. We were not created to conform, we were created to be transformed into the image of God. Conforming will make us disappear. Conforming will make the characteristics and presence of our God disappear, until God chooses to manifest and become judge and jury of the frauds that we have become.

Life is a journey that requires a roadmap for navigation. Unless you are connected to the Creator of life, you may find yourself lost in a world of imitation and emulation, constantly changing masks, one persona to another but never evolving. You were made for individuality. You were made for a unique purpose. You were made to imitate one and one alone; our Divine Creator and it is important to know that without this connection, you will remain lost. That is the purpose of this book. It is amidst the pages of this book that you will discover that you are lost, but have been found. It is within the pages of this book that you will discover, if for the first time, that the knowledge of your current wanderings is the first step in changing the trajectory of your life. For once you will realize your obscurity, you can then become intentional about life navigation. This book is different as within its pages is poetic heart centered dialogue that exemplifies the complexity of this life. It is my sincerest hope that the pages within this book you will find your own thoughts, identify with questions posed, and find some solutions to help you along your own journey. More importantly, it is my prayer that these words increase your courage and motivation to live a life of focused intention and connection with God, and with the authentic you that was pre-destined for this moment, this day, the season, and this life. It is my prayer that as you walk through each of the chapters within this navigational tool, that you will see yourself differently, you will gain an understanding that you … is now we because you are never apart from God. Intrinsically designed by divine hands, and deliberately crafted with such precision, and love, the world is waiting to behold you! So what are you waiting for, let's meet the one whom God envisioned, and entrusted his image too! Let's walk together, with God, on this journey of the heart.

Table of CONTENTS

PREFACE: A Letter to the Inner Me V
ACKNOWLEDGMENTS VII
EPIGRAPH IX
THE SYMPTOM of Being You: XI
CHAPTER 1: Discovering I was lost 1
CHAPTER 2: The Revealing 17
CHAPTER 3: The Journey of the Heart 31
CHAPTER 4: The Encounter: I AM 59
CHAPTER 5: Learning How to Dwell 77
CHAPTER 6: My Daily Walk with Intention 100
CHAPTER 7: From Bitter to Beautiful 110
CHAPTER 8: Living Truth 131
CHAPTER 9: Aligned and Synergized 149
CHAPTER 10: Unconditional Love 169
EPILOGUE 189
BIOGRAPHY 191
CONNECT WITH Sha'Leda Mirra On Social Media 193
ENDNOTES 195

Chapter 1:
DISCOVERING I WAS LOST

At the verge of annihilation in God, there seems to be a region of sweet confusion, the sense of being in many places at once, saying multiple sentences. A hazy melting, fragile, and nearly blank. Profound ignorance, within which conventional, calm behavior seems insane!

~Rumi[4]

It's in the confusion that you lose YOU!

I Almost Disappeared

I ALMOST DISAPPEARED. Every remnant of me was slowly fading away, as I morphed into something unknown.

As I allowed your wants, your desires, your challenges, your criticism, your praises and your degradations to make me run and hide.

To make me covet someone else's life.

That made me want to lock up my diamonds and rubies that have been purified, by the creator of life.

I missed the message: that I am created in the image of the grand architect of the Universe.

The only message I received, is that no matter how often I changed my masks to appease you …

Every time, I walked away questioning.

Every time, I walked away insecure.

Every time, I walked away broken.

Every time, I walked away, less of me, more of … something else … someone else.

I looked foreign when I looked in the mirror at myself~ Who are you? Why are you here?

The more I conformed to oblige you, guising it as selflessness, calling it my contribution to humanity, the stranger I looked; and my feelings became intensely foreign.

As I put off my desires, goals, and dreams to follow the road map that you developed for me;

As I placed your opinions in such a place of prestige, so esteemed that your voice became my voice, and my voice I could barely hear.

My motto became, *"what would the world do?"* I was in you; I breathed you, I supped with you, I drank of you … and you still did not accept me.

So, then, I began to wonder ... what is it about me? This totally conformable, transformable, positively perpetrating, chameleon that can, almost instantaneously, be anything and everything you need me to be; and, yet, you still renounce me as if I am nothing at all?

Then, I read this verse, and the spell was broken off my mind.

> *"But you are a chosen people, a royal priesthood, a holy nation, God's special possession, that you declare the praises of Him who called you out of darkness into his wonderful light."*
>
> ~1 Peter 2:9[5]

I'm chosen?
I'm royal?
I'm holy?
I'm special?

That's not what they say as I lay my head on the pillow, wearied from the days toils.

The next day I woke up, and looked in the mirror. I was not there, just a reflection of what should of, or what could of, but not what *is*.

And, I thought, as I stood in overwhelm, with the stranger in my house staring back at me from the steam filled mirror;

We exhaust so much energy trying to make ourselves visible to others.

We, daily, seek to impress those in whom we come into contact by our immense vernacular, our monumental achievements, our outer adornments and dress.

We abandon our divine dream, encapsulated and embodied in our essence, as we transitioned from life eternal to life now mortal; in order to chase the worldly dream.

We change-a chameleon in an ever changing environment.

We have more faces and personas than colors reflected in nature.

Man made, clones, of our external delights.

We become … .others … .instead of ourselves.

Perplexed, I pondered … Why do we spend so much time trying to be visible to others when we are invisible to ourselves?

Is it possible for others to see what we cannot see?

All this internal dialogue was enough to cause overwhelming fatigue. The days came and they went. I felt no substance, I felt nothing…

On the final day, I awakened from what appeared to be a delusion that lasted several decades. On this day, I was beside myself, and again, I examined myself and realized that I did not recognize me. It's a peculiar thing not to recognize your own skin. Then, in my subconscious recollection, I hear a voice uttering R.H. Sin's poem, "My Own Stranger," where he defined it best that sometimes when we consult the keeper of our own reflection, we don't recognize self.

The eyes that are the mirror to our soul have become convoluted and disillusioned with the perceptions of others.

So much so, that it will become your reality. It was mine.

But there was something different about today!

Because, on this day, I began to pray; and I discovered that I was lost.

A whisper spoke so gently and said, "Come unto me," and, I could see myself, I could feel myself; and the most divine revelation happened. In that moment, I recognized God, and I also recognized me ... for the first time.

So foreign yet so peaceful. God felt nothing like my reality.

I realized I had been called out of the darkness and into the light by His great pleasure. Beams of bright light and angelic voices radiated around me. I once was lost, but now, I am found.

I almost disappeared.

But, God found me, and led me to me!

We are not our own:

JEREMIAH 10:23 STATES, *"Lord, I know that people's lives are not their own; it is not for them to direct their steps."* [6] My dear friends, this is why we are lost. Somewhere along the way, someone convinced us that we are the masters of our own fate, the architect of our existence, and the compass that guides our path. Somewhere along the way, someone fed us the fabrications that we have all of the answers to every question, the solution to every problem, and knowledge to set the trajectory, lead, and direct our own path in life. I stand to blow the whistle on the mendacity of this demonic tactic. Scripture is clear that we, as humans, are not our own, and we are not equipped to direct our steps. So, if we are not equipped, then who is? We can consult the writings of one of the major prophets, Isaiah, (Isaiah 29:14-16), states the following words that describe our desire for lordship in our own lives:

> *"Therefore once more, I will astound these people with wonder upon wonder; the wisdom of the wise will perish, the intelligence of the intelligent will vanish. Woe to those who go to great depths to hide their plans from the Lord, who do their work in darkness and think 'who sees us? Who will know?' You turn things upside down as if the potter were thought to be like the clay! Shall what is formed say to the one who formed it, 'you did not make me?' Can the pot say to the potter, 'you know nothing?'"* [7]

This is, in fact, what we do everyday when we refuse to allow God to reign supreme in our lives. Instead of yielding to God, asking for His divine revelation and guidance, we become the clay giving direction to the potter, when, in fact, we are not, nor will we ever be, equipped to give God instruction on those whom God created in His image. The key to finding ourselves is understanding that we "are not our own, we were bought at a price'" and if we want to find ourselves, we must first find the creator. Each of us, every human who exists or has ever existed, God foreknew. God is the only one with the power to create. Romans 8:29-30 tells us that *"for those God foreknew, He also predestined to be conformed to the image of His son, that he might be the first born among many brothers and sisters. And those He predestined, He also called; those He called, He also justified; those He justified, He also glorified."* [8] God has all the answers to every question you have, every plaguing problem, and every solution you seek. Don't lose yourself by believing you are the lord of your life. God is the only one that can allow holistic transformation and divine confirmation, so that you can meet and build a relationship with the authentic you. However it is important to remember that on the journey to becoming, you will have scars, for they are the evidence that you walked through the wilderness, and are now triumphant.

Scars:

> "Our scars are our deepest stories. They tell of the wounds that brought us to this moment, and remind us that even the tough stuff we are walking through now will one day heal. Scars tell the stories of our past; inspiring others to find beauty in their wounds." – Becky Hurting[9]

YOUR SCARS TELL the beauty of the story that is you.

Each scar is attached to a memory, not of pain, not of heartache,

But, of resilience, to overcoming, to internal strength you never thought you possessed.

Cheers to you.

Can you change your perception for a moment and see the positively healed side of you?

Can you look beyond your pain and see the beckoning call of the one who is stronger, wiser?

Can you see the one who holds the world and all that is in His hands?

If you can, then you know there is strength in weakness.

For God says, "When you are weak, I am strong."

Why then do we endeavor to use every form of make-up to cover up the testimony that can bring healing to thousands.

As if, our disclosure will cause unbearable shame and harm.

Un-masking is the most significant form of self-validation, because at that moment, you assert to the world that you have fallen in love with God and the most important person, the one that matters most.

ME, because though separate, God resides in me.

Your scars triggered awareness that conversion was necessary.

Your scars, led to your surrender.

Your surrender led you to God.

In Him, you can now live, move, and enjoy your being, your life; and smile.

Knowing that in your weakest moment,

In your vulnerable moment,

In your shame ridden moment,

In your most painful moment,

You gained freedom, and power. You were launched into new life.

What a gift, to be transformed from the inside-out, so that others witness the beauty that you exude inside OUT.

Your scars led you to a place of healing that wasn't isolated, but holistic … Salubrious.

The healing power of God; synergy with He who was, is, and is yet to come,

Transformed you, so that you can now reflect Him.

Your Scars. God's Healing. Tell the story that is you.

It takes courage to conceptualize the dilemma.

The Dilemma:

AS A THERAPIST and a pastor, I have had the unique opportunity to work with many individuals whom, on the outside, have no deformations, no scars, and present a picture of success and health. They schedule an appointment, dress in their best clothing, both internal and external, and sit on my chair in a state of phantasm, with a miraged countenance-the epitomal reflection of fraud. Hiding behind their counter-factual lives. During the rapport process, they externally engage in an internal debate, trying to audibly convince themselves that everything is okay. They forget that I too am in the room, observing, listening. In this setting, the subconscious seems to take control, which immediately reduces one's self or conscious control. This interpersonal ruction lasts for almost an hour, as I watch them, talk to themselves as if they had just met themselves for the first time. Sitting quietly in the dimly lit room, I allow them to combat the duality of voices that triggers the confused bifold nature that has shaped the person that talks back to them. Two voices, one person. Two perceptions, one mind. Invisible scars, visibly seen because all the make-up was washed away by the waterfall of their tears. One person can have two natures. One person can drift between reality and make-believe. This is why Christ states that we cannot follow Him and be in the world. The mind wasn't meant to process two perceptions. We chastize our children about building monuments of existence that we say is far from reality. Guess what … adults do it too. For some it's called pretending, but for many, it's called coping.

And to both the pretending and the coping we have become numb.

These repeated episodes prompted me to examine my own scars. As I explored my own personal scars, I realized that, though, to the naked eye, the scars appeared to be healed, underneath the superficial layer of the epidermis, healing was still in progress. There were times when the trauma enacted pain that was too strong to bear. The present intensity of an aged long experience from life's past, still possessed the ability to resurface in my mind; and at times, with such intensity, that it possessed the power to completely arrest every emotion, every thought, every action, every conscious and subconscious response. As I would sit for moments that are so paralyzing, they felt like days, I realized that I must give myself permission to, in this moment, process the pain so that I can heal. Questions plagued my mind. Why does society make us feel that we must hide what hurts? Why is it normal to hide? Why is retreat and escape more appealing than problem solving? Have we become creatures of darkness, exposing to the light only what we think the light should see? Why is it an anathema for me to say that I am suffering, distressed, wounded, marred, and aggrieved?

Why can I not scream, "Help!" and expect someone to come to my rescue? Why is it so debilitating to free ourselves of the prison of suppressed emotional responses, and pretend that we are holistically healthy and whole? Rumi[10] asks the question, "Why do you stay in prison when the door is so wide open?" Why have I spent so much time trying to heal from the outside-in, instead of the inside-out? Why are we, as a society, so hypervigilantly focused on the scars that are visible to others, instead of the healing the invisible scar that is within? Why is prioritizing internal healing taboo, but external healing is promoted? Is there anything wrong with allowing tears so they can cleanse the soul?

I began to cry. Holding my tears reminded me that tears like storms, precipitate water that comes to wash away the facade. I allowed myself to feel ... myself.

In your world of make believe, I need you to know, the make-up washes off. Maybe that's why you could never stand the rain. Maybe you need to stand outside on a stormy day, to cleanse yourself ... of yourself.

Water is necessary for the washing, and for the purifying of your soul. Water removes the outward impurities so that the inward soul can be seen, so that it can be healed. We must, however, shift our focus from simply trying to remove the dirt from our physical body and the soot from our reputation; and ask the Spirit of the living water to wash the dirt from your soul. This is the only way we can have a clear conscience towards God and expect to commune with Him.

> *"And this water symbolizes baptism that now saves you also, not the removal of dirt from the body but the pledge of a clear conscience towards God." −1 Peter 3:21[11].*

Yet many still refuse the opportunity to shed the tear out of fear.
And even still, they refuse to drink the Living water for an inward fill that will divinely reveal.

Instead they choose to sit on my chair, scarred internally and bitter that no one even noticed the pain. And, because of their scars, their entire perception of the world changed. Make-up-make-believe, became their reality. Living outside-in, instead of inside-out.

On most days they stand at the door thinking, there is no need to go outside.

I concur. The real change starts with-IN.

But don't hide. Find God.

Or else, you become a montage.

The Montage:

Montage

noun

the technique of combining in a single composition pictorial elements from various sources, as parts of different photographs or fragments of printing, either to give the illusion that the elements belonged together originally or to allow each element to retain its separate identity as a means of adding interest or meaning to the composition.[12]

WE REFLECT A montage every day that we place ourselves on the throne designed only for the infinite and the grand designer of all things.

Why do I say this? Because, every day of our lives we are reflecting some attribute, some characteristic, some behavior.

Illuminating some light, or maybe a montage that presents as light, but instead, is darkness guised as light.

If the light is not a ray that is reflected from the light of the world, Our Savior, then the reflection is only a montage;

Giving the illusion of one thing, a buttress of facade ... An apparition, a hoax, an imitation, a counterfeit.

Why expend so much energy morphing into the faulty design of another?

Abandoning introspection, and, yet, chasing after and modeling the creation of another; who, when you search for the inception of their ethos—our ethos, your ethos—you find that they, too, are just another semblance of another.

How easy it is for us to get lost in the sea of persona ... The montage.

All the while, abandoning self for approval.

Why a montage?

Approval-Addiction

WHAT IS APPROVAL addiction? Being overly anxious and obsessed with the opinion and acceptance of another human, just like you.

Infused with a compulsion to be what you feel others need or want you to be.

Buying into the lie and the dangling bait of Satan.

Bait that embeds thoughts into your mind that you are not enough; not good enough, not smart enough, not pretty enough, not talented enough.

That to become anything special, or to become anyone of worth, you must abandon SELF and embark upon a quest of enlightenment that reveals to you, that you are not you; and that to transcend to nobility and godliness, you must first cease to be you.

And who, then, do you become? You become one; self-seeking and placing yourself on the illusion of a throne, knowing that the throne was never created for you. Fighting to prove your worth to a lost society who could never understand you.

Ruth Chou Simmons stated it best in her work, "Graceland."

> *"When I trace every anxious thought back to its origin, I inevitably find my fear of failure and need for approval waiting for me. I want to be the prettiest, smartest, or best because I think securing these will give me the confidence and assurance I crave. But, they don't."* [13]

From where did this notion derive?

That in order to be anything of worth and or value that we must, then, become the dictator of our character.

And, that our life's purpose is to find the right for our wrong, the good for our bad, the present for our missing, the sufficiency for our lack.

This quest is not entirely wrong; for there is an answer to every question that plagues man, and a remedy for the ills of our sin.

But, it can be found no other place than God. Yet, God is the last that we seek.

We become fixated on the creatED and not the creatOR.

When did we become indoctrinated with such a warped sense of self-concept? I mean, this must have taken us by surprise.

When did we join hands with those who do not trust that God knew exactly what He was doing when He created us? When did we become so willing to give ourselves over to the mores of this world, seeking a rebirth.

Seeking to be re-created by the hands of others who have no power to create, refine, define, or assign …

Purpose.

Then, I remembered something that we must remember … The enemy cannot create, he can only produce a montage.

So who are you? Are you who God has called you to be?
Or, are you what the world has conditioned you to be?

I realized that conformity was a symptom of a larger issue: our own montage.
And, then, God spoke, and reality set in.
God said, "Choose me. Or else, exist as a montage."

Before God will reveal, we must first courageously admit, Lord, I am lost!

Chapter 2:
THE REVEALING

Creation has value for both God and humanity in a dialectical way. For God, there is the joy of self-expression and interpersonal communication. God is delighted by the way that nature can mirror the divine and exhibit its traces.[14]

-Carl Pinnock

I must learn to mirror the divine.

The Miss-Education of Me

In a world where expectation seems to be everything,
I find that there are many who think they know me, but they, in fact, only know what they expect of me.

They spend so much time in observation, but no time in interaction; and based on this distorted perception, they investigate me through an obscurely tainted lens, formulating an ideal, a persona, that they assign to me.

It is their own reality, their own version, pieced together, fragmented with frantically and secretly sought out snippets of information, written with the tool of their imagination.

They then assign a name, a body; and even though they know it's not the same, the feelings, yet, remain, and they call this form by my name,

and then, project she onto me.

This masterpiece, as others see, is not me …

It's your miss-education of me.

My Subconscious Fight for Freedom

AN INTERNAL DIALOGUE:

> I desire that my subconscious spews forth, like vomit from the innermost part of me. Spewing all of the toxins from within that have kept me slave to a past I forgot … Or at least, I thought.

A benighted slave. But, yet, I yell, "freedom." Silly me!

Atticus once wrote, "Her heart was wild, but I didn't want to catch it. I wanted to run with it to set mine free."[15] For me, in this moment, there is no truer -ism to describe my desire to break free from the bond that has grabbed ahold of me and left me standing stagnant, chasing distractions, as if they are the key to all that

I long for. Wild and free, is the opposite; an oxymoron of sorts, when you compare current reality to my dream of who I could be and where I should be. There are some things that I have asked for in the silent sinews of my heart, and had it not been for God saying no, and His divine prevention that barred me from walking through the forbidden door, I would have dug a grave for me that was so deep, there would have been no way of escape. It was God's willful ignorance of me, as I tried to play tug of war, that opened my eyes in the valley experience called NO. Here I sit with myself, within myself, with a burning desire to put pen to paper, my finger to the stroke of a keyboard, writing; which is exactly what God told me to do in the first place. The key to setting my soul free is not wrapped tightly in freeing others; that is my deflection. It is in exposing myself to the freedom that I chase, and introducing it to others. Yet, how can I lead someone down a path that I, myself, seek to escape the trod? Why can I not allow my heart to be free-so wild, that it cannot be caught? Why can't we all be wild horses?

They say ... because, God made you in His image, and bearing that image has divine expectations. God says, whom the Son sets free, is free in deed. But freedom requires authenticity.

So, why, then, have you halted in place? And, why so dreary the face? Why have you stalled in the race; and why, your potential, do you forsake? Why did you stop and dream in the day; and at night, your thoughts, vivid and unrelenting, you can't help but lie awake? Why have you chosen this place in life; but in your subconscious reality, you yearn for freedom?

Isn't that pretending?

We live in this fairytale world of expectation. Someone along the way told us that the key to happiness was wrapped up in pretending. Pretending, you may ask … ? Yes! Pretending! Pretending is to function in an altered reality without authenticity. You pretend that you want to wake up every morning and go to work. While on your job, you pretend you want to be there. You pretend to like everyone around you, when, in fact, the core of you wishes that some of them did not even exist in your world. You pretend to see things you did not see; this is so eloquently guised in the masking of your elaborate gossip and expansive altered stories. Then, there are times when you pretend you do not see, turning your attention away from the experienced wrong, and quelling your voice and quenching your inner advocacy. You pretend you have enough resources to meet all of your needs. You pretend to be happy, when, in fact, you long for more as you lay down to sleep, with a deep desire to escape by staying asleep.

So many of us are sleepwalking in the day … .
Wake UP.

The Truth

BEFORE THE FOUNDATIONS of the earth, God knew you. God had you on God's mind. God predestined you and pre-ordained you for a specific purpose in this life. Just imagine God with a pencil and paper as God sat down to construct you. God orchestrated everything about who you are: past, present, future, and beyond. The humanity and eternity of you, God wrote it all. God trusted you with His purpose. And, even though God knew that there would be times that you would sleep-walk, journeying in willful ignorance, He believed that with your free-will, you would freely choose to accept, love, and serve Him. So, what happens when the purpose is not served? You were created for synchrony with only God's thoughts and God's purpose. Any other function, any other role, is deemed outside of God's will. The epitome of pretending is when you are everyone doing everything other than what God called you to be and do. You look foreign to God. Failing to reflect God's image means that you have settled for impersonation of the created versus the creator. IDOLATRY. Without God's purpose, there is nothing to fulfill, and you will never be fulfilled until you purge your will and seek the freedom that only God can give. God is the granter of authenticity. God speaks to the soul and subconscious parts of us, and creates divine alignment. It is in the subconscious where God speaks, that our freedom lives.

Why the subconscious? This is a resting place and the playground of the mind. It is the place where authenticity lies. It is the place where you can uninhibitedly live. It is the place with the least restrictions, and where our dreams and desires live. This is the place where God can commune with humankind at will, without our efforts to control, rationalize, judge, and direct. Why do we, as humanity, feel like self-control versus sacrifice to God is the way? Why are we so afraid of freedom? Maybe it's in our fleshly chaos that we find our true self. Spirit, beautifully wrapped in a lack of normalcy, odd peculiarity, royally defiant to the world, but in alignment with God. Authentic. Intentional. Aligned.

I Long for New

ONE OF THE ways that I prefer to cope with the stressors of life is to shop. It's not an impulsivity or an addiction, but yet, a desire to attain newness. There is something comforting, something exciting, something fresh about acquiring the new. A new outfit has the ability to make us feel like a new person; someone different, as if we have escaped some situation or condition that defines us, setting us free each time, as if it was the first time. Many of us recite the scripture often that each day brings new mercies, new excitements, and new opportunities. I say, this is only recited by the progressively minded, as many look for the yesterday in their today. Reality is, we are so busy looking back, that there is minimal forward progression. Have you ever tried to walk forward while you are looking backward? If you have tried, odds are, you found it quite difficult. You are unable to see what was in front of you, when your body is shifted forward, but your head is shifted to the rear. You cannot possibly move forward or achieve any progression if all of your energies are exhausted with analyzing and problem solving the past.

This is why newness is so attractive to us. We desire spiritually, mentally, emotionally, psychologically, physiologically, and intellectually-A NEW START! A do-over. The opportunity to redeem ourselves from past mishaps that we think have ruined the course of life for us. We are looking for redemption. We are looking to prove ourselves to the naysayers, for fulfilling the very reality they prophesied for us. How often we unknowingly make someone else's expectation our self-fulfilling prophecy. Keeping our mind fixed on the complexities of yesterday, grants others the power and permission to dig holes deep enough to plant a seed that will take root in our lives. If we are not careful, we water the seeds planted within us by others, and reap the harvest of their desire. In looking back, you re-present yourself over and over again to the well of death. You share dreams and visions with those who you thought were in your corner; yet, they secretly prayed for the dreams you shared to vanish and amount to nothing.

Why did you allow those who were around you to re-define your purpose? Why did you allow them to establish the borders and parameters of your heart? Why did you allow them to taint the vision; coloring your glasses with the tinted paint of their choosing, coloring your perception and expectation of life? Who told you that this was the right way? Where did you learn that deceptively manipulative behavior was okay? You, the past pieces of you, allowed the essence of your soul to be placed as a sheet of paper under the pen of another who was never meant to have a part in coloring in the unshaded and unfinished pieces of you. They were never meant to possess a tool that had the capacity of rewriting a story that you never even began; a story that is only revealed through connection with God.

Without a connection with the Almighty Creator, you have no story. Your legacy is non-existent. Your presence is meaningless. Who you are is absent. You are a piece with no matching puzzle. You are the stage set for a miraculous play with no actors. You are a weed in the middle of the grassfield. You are chaff that is blown away with the wind.

There is danger in an unhealthy, internal connection to the past, because this is the enemies way of destroying your future. By keeping you overcome in the condemnation attached to past choices, you are chasing wind. The enemy specializes in keeping you focused on what you cannot change-the circumstance, which inhibits what can be changed, which is you ... for the future. Sometimes, this means you must go somewhere new. When I am somewhere new, expectations do not exist. I am allowed to explore and define who I am. I am allowed to enjoy experiences moment by moment, without explanation. God makes all things new. New becomes the eraser that has been activated on the chalkboard of my past, because it is easier for me to move past my past, where there are not constant, external reminders of it.

I long for new. This means I must purge myself ... of myself. Soul detox.

Detoxification and Purging

As we walk through life, there are so many poisonous and virulent toxins that we can (unknowingly) ingest that have the potential of being harmful, or even lethal to our health. Therefore, it is of the utmost importance that we pay close attention to what we allow ourselves to listen to, watch, touch, and smell. At the moment of contact, exposure occurs. Exposure comes by being in a particular place, at a particular time. Exposure is symbolic of connection whether desired or not; and being in that place is, in most instances, a choice. Before you embark on any journey, whether short distances or longer distances, you must ask yourself, "have I spent the necessary time in preparation for the journey?" Sure, we spend time making sure that we have packed the appropriate clothes, toiletries, and even food or snacks, but did we prepare for our emotional and spiritual needs to ensure that we are fully prepared for what awaits us upon arrival? How often we think we are prepared and show up in the arena, fully exposed for attack; beautifully arrayed in our physical clothing, but our spiritual clothing that provides the most protection, leaves us exposed, and bare for all to see, and for the enemy to begin to prey. We, so willingly, walk into life's toxins, ungirded, and ignorant of the poison that kills us slowly, while the enemy watches in sheer delight from afar. Then, we find our circumstances so offensive, that we blame God for allowing an attack upon us, when it was us that failed to get into His presence, seek His guidance, and allow Him to anoint and prepare us for what lies ahead. O what a difference it would make if we could, and we would, before making any decisions within our day, pack with preparation for our spiritual and emotional needs. This spiritual preparation is more than just praying for what we want and need, but all the more, we must detoxify our lives through the process of purging and be vigilant about exposure time.

What does it mean to purge?

PURGE MEANS: TO rid self of an unwanted feeling, memory, or condition. Words synonymous with purge to ensure clarity are: to cleanse, clear, purify, wash, eject, remove, or get rid of. Purging gives a sense of cathartic release. Cathartic release is attached to a psychological relief; meaning that what we rid ourselves of, places us in a healthier state physically, emotionally, and spiritually. It is healthy, then, to purge ourselves of the many toxins that are the byproducts of unwholesome talk, unhealthy connections and attachments, lying, lustful thoughts, and unhealthy eating habits, in order to achieve a personal spiritual catharsis. We must release and expel from our being, which has been declared a holy temple of God, everything that might serve to promote illness.

Illness is a direct result of toxic overload. Illness, resultant from toxins, occurs because of the exposure time to the toxins. If, after an encounter, we would immediately detoxify self through holistic purging, we would find that illness may not be our lot. But, if the exposure time increases, and we fail to purge ourselves immediately from that which so hazardously permeates our environment, we may then experience the ill effects to our body, mind, and spirit.

One of the most jeopardous positions we can find ourselves in, is willful ignorance. Willful ignorance is the after-effect of a life that is misaligned or quite simply out of alignment with God. God would not have us ignorant, especially of the devices of the enemy; and, therefore, alignment and time in the presence of Almighty God is the key. We are not omniscient or omnipresent, and thus, we are limited in our knowing and being. However, we serve a God who is all knowing and occupies a place in ages past and yet remains our hope for the future. God will, through repeated exposure to HIM, warn us of the toxins, whether it be people, places, or things, so that we will not be ignorant in our daily lives. We need the illumination and exposure of the Holy Spirit to increase our discerning knowledge, so that we can avoid the many toxic traps created for us by the accuser of the brethren. When we are aligned with God, we are the epitome of what is referred to by the Apostle Peter, as sober and vigilant, because the adversary is ever looking for ways to devour your life, and spirit (1 Peter 5:8)[16].

So, you may be asking how do I detoxify my life? How do I begin the process of purging myself from the toxins that so easily lead to illness due to exposure overload? Below are a few tips:

Alignment with God. Alignment with God comes through prayer and connection. You must make time, daily, to get into the presence of Almighty God. This can include prayer, study of scripture, meditation on God's word, and listening to His instructions to you. If you do not purpose to synergize with God daily, you will be mis-aligned and ignorant concerning the exposure of dangerous toxins in the natural and supernatural.

Surrender to the will of God. Sin, which is prolonged exposure to our fleshly desires and will, results in illness and, ultimately, eternal death. Sin happens when we are busy chasing our will, and not God's will. We must abandon our will and sacrifice ourselves at the altar of Almighty God, surrendering holistically to Him. Nothing else will do! Surrendering to God's will is the greatest sacrifice you will ever make.

Remain Exposed to God and He will protect you from toxic overload. This means you must be obedient and yield to the unction of the Holy Spirit. The Holy Spirit's purpose is to lead and guide, which means, you are never without a leader who will guide you in the way. The position of leadership in your life must be given to God, and then, you must willingly allow Him to guide you. Remember, you are not your own. You were bought with a price. The toxic sin of man led to our Savior being crucified on a cross, and yet, it is only through His shed blood that we obtain the remission from the blood stained toxins of sin that, if not purged, will lead us to eternal death. Jesus Exposure, protects you from toxic exposure.

Obey. God will communicate healthy ways for you to detoxify your mind, body, and spirit. Whether it be a diet change, job change, a vacation, other methods for wellness, and spending more time walking and talking with you, know that all things are at God's disposal to use concerning His care for you! Once He communicates what is needed, be swift in obedience to His commands.

With all of the toxins we encounter daily that impact our emotional, physical, and spiritual health, it is important that we prioritize detoxification. It is in the purging and detoxing that God begins to pull back the layers hiding us, revealing the new YOU that God created before time even existed. It is only in a state of purity that God can reveal what can only been seen through spiritual eyes. Can you see what God is revealing?

The Revealing:

Message to Humanity~A Monologue

I worked hard to reveal me. I wanted to reveal me, but all you wanted to see was you. I mean, the parts of you that were complete because my presence filled a void in you and inspired you to be who you desired to be.

Did you not care that as I filled you up, you left me empty? Left me famished–a drought drier than the Sahara Desert. As lifeless as the ocean when the earth stops turning on its axis.

I sometimes talk to myself and wonder, how could I spend so much time studying the curriculum of you; and yet, realize, at the end of the course, you didn't know me ... at all?

You failed the test of intimacy, the test of compatibility, the test of desirability; you failed, and, yet, you sit and stare, smirking as if you didn't even care.

Life provides us with opportunities to show up in the uniqueness of who we are. We desire to show up, naked, unclothed.

We desire to meet someone, achieve the highest level of interaction, which is companionship.

We desire to know that someone, anyone, accepts us with no additions, no changes, no prefacing, no buts, no what ifs.

Just me.

And, yet ... I'm still searching ... I think I have found her. In all the earth, is there only one?

Thank you, God, for the revealing. Hello ME!

"At every ending, there is a beginning; and maybe, just maybe, we should long for the ending, so that we can look for the new journey of the heart, wherein lies the heart of God."

– Sha'Leda Mirra

Chapter 3:
THE JOURNEY OF THE HEART

Thomas Merton states, "We love to clothe this false self . . . and I wind experiences around myself with pleasures and glory like bandages in order to make myself visible to myself and to the world, as if I were an invisible body that could only become visible when something visible covered its surface. But, there is no substance under the things with which I am clothed. I am hollow. . . And, when they are gone, there will be nothing left of me but my own nakedness and emptiness and hollowness."[17]

If I don't make it a priority to find me, who will? So I have decided today, my journey is to turn aside and connect with the heart of God. Deciding is one thing, manifestation is another.

Why am I standing still?

With so much of the world to see, and so much created to satiate my inner curiosity,

Why am I so content with mediocrity? Why am I standing still?

In my thoughts, I dream and long to be free from my daily song that keeps me trapped all day long.

Buried by the expectations of those other than me.

I know I must work in order to play.

I know that I must plan to know the way.

And, yet, with all I do today,

I still find myself standing still.

I want to be on the back of the eagle.

Flying higher moment by moment.

I want to be greater, still.

Yet, I can't seem to allow my feet to lift off the ground.

I'm in a place where the dreams are so vivid and real.

And, yet, there is still a part of me that fears.

God is saying, the time has now passed when it was obedient to be still;

And, I need you to run all the way.

The wait is over.

I have given you the strength.

I have given you the vision.

I have given you the financial support.

I have given you the gifting.

I've given you the desire, that is tugging at your soul to go higher. So, you are without excuse, my child, to, yet, be standing still.

Prepare to shift.

The heart-centered journey requires the deepest degree of self-exploration imaginable. It requires exploring what we deem as patterns of normalcy to discover if it is normal. During this exploration, confessions of the darkest secrets will occur. Inner conflict will trigger storms unimaginable. Exposure of unhealed scars, thought healed, will begin to ache, again. All of this is necessary for healing to occur. All of this is necessary for transformation to overtake us and shift us into becoming. Becoming what, you may ask? Becoming who God designed you to be. Allow me to take you on a journey of the heart.

The Journey of the Heart

JAMES K.A. SMITH once penned these words that ring true for every human alive: "To be human, is to be on a quest. To live, is to be embraced on a kind of journey toward a destination of your dreams."[18] Whether we want to admit it or not, we are all journeying somewhere. Some of us are attuned to our heart's center, the place where God resides, and others are simply drifting to a destination unknown. My question to you is, what does your destiny look like? Where is your *telos*, your end destination? Have you allowed the vision for your life to emanate from your heart, or are you lost in a sea of nothingness, hoping that someone might be so kind as to lead you to where they think you should be? In this chapter, we are going to delve deep into a comparative analysis of these two quests. We will examine each, intricately, so that you walk away with an understanding of the urgency of knowing that the course of your journey will lead you to life or to death. There is nothing more dangerous than a human soul, created in the image of a sovereign and Holy God, sojourning, alone, to a destination unknown.

"The glory of God is man, fully alive." ~ St. Ireneaus[19]

From the moment that we are born, we are ingrained with everything; every tool, every bit of knowledge and wisdom to make it to your divine destination. In fact, I assert that we know God intimately before we are given a journey of humanity. I can safely assume this because of scriptures, such as that of Jeremiah 1:5, states, "Before I formed you in the womb, I knew you. Before you were born, I set you apart; I appointed you as a prophet to the nations."[20] Psalms 139:13 propounds the validity of the same message given to the prophet Jeremiah. "For you created my innermost being; you knit me together in my mother's womb."[21] This means, that before you were released into the realm of humanity, God created a storyline for your life! God began to narrate your purpose, your destiny; and inside your heart, your soul and spirit, God planted his seed that should manifest into your heart-centered journey. Why did I say that it should manifest? The reality is, that while all is perfect in the heavenly realm, and God created His divinely intimate plan for each of us, He is also keenly aware that we were birthed into a world of evil. God the Father, and Jesus the son, and the sweet communion of the Holy Spirit, are very well aware of the tests, trials, and temptations that will greet you from the moment the seed of the man is supplanted in the uterine wall of the woman. While the egg is in the womb for the purpose of being nurtured, we see, even before birth, the embryo feasting on the environmental exposure of the mother and the father; less reliant on the hands of God, and at the mercy of parental choices. This seedling, is also being exposed to the tactics of the enemy who begins his attack at the very moment of conception. What I love most about God, is that while He understands that our lives will not be perfect and that we will be exposed to the filth of this life that seeks to slowly kill what He has created, He, yet, decides to send us on this journey. He doesn't send us on this journey without provisions and protections. Even at the most helpless of states, God has equipped us with all that we will need to have life and have it more abundantly.

Though we are divinely pre-equipped, somewhere between eternity and finite humanity, we lose the most divine aspects of ourselves. I liken this transition from the cradle and heart of God, to morality as that which we see in the scripture, Philipians 2:7. I am in no way equating humanity to God, but if we view the process of our birth and our conception, we understand that we were alive with God the Father, Christ the Son, and the Holy Spirit before we were born, even if it was only as a concept or plan in the heart and mind of God. Isn't this what is spoken to Jeremiah? "Before I formed you in the womb, I knew you. Before you were born I set you apart; I appointed you as a prophet to the nations."[22] (Jeremiah 1:5) If that isn't enough proof of our existence with God before our humanity, let's also examine Galatians 1:5, where we see Paul making his case about God's predestined and pre-ordained plan for his life, even when he was unaware. Paul states, "But when God, who set me apart from my mother's womb and called me by His grace, was pleased to reveal His Son in me, so that I might preach Him among the gentiles, my immediate response was not to consult any human being."[23] Why did Paul not feel the need to consult any other human being? Paul, in this passage, had come to the realization that God was the source and finish of his life; God was His telos. Paul realized, in this moment, that God's plan was his ultimate purpose in life. Can humanity (those made in the image of God) dictate another's purpose, plan, and the way that he should walk along this journey? Paul further states in Romans 9: 20-21, "But who are you, a human being, to talk back to God? Shall what is formed say to the one who formed it, why did you make me like this? Does not the potter have the right to make out of the same lump of clay pottery for special purposes and some for common use?"[24] What Paul is stating here is, only God, only the creator, knows the reason why He created us. Only God knows and can reveal our purpose. Can man be used as a tool of God to confirm our purpose? Sure. But, remember, the revelation still came from God.

One more scripture to propound our existence with our God before this mortal existence is Psalms 139: 13-16. "For you formed my inward parts; you knitted me together in my mother's womb. I praise you, for I am fearfully and wonderfully made. Wonderful are your works; my soul knows it very well. My frame was not hidden from you, when I was being made in secret, intricately woven in the depths of the earth. Your eyes saw my unformed substance; in your book were written, every one of them the days that were formed for me, when as yet there was none of them."[25] Isn't this powerful? Isn't this divine? To know that each of us existed with our God before we were yet in human form. This should be enough to support our existence with God before our birth, and through His atoning works on the cross, we have the opportunity to return to our origin; into the hands of the Father who created us. We have the opportunity to return from whence we came. Home!

So, back to our original message. We were exploring the separation that happens from divine immortality into sinful mortal humanity. There is a separation that occurs when God plants the seed into man and it is conceived in the woman. That, which once belonged to God, is placed in this sinful world; but not without provision for all that we will need for this journey of life. You see, God allows us to travel the journey of life because He desires to know … will you freely choose Him? Will you forsake all others? Will you forsake the pleasures of mortality to live with Him eternally? The journey through life is the only way to achieve the crown of immortality. The journey through life is the test that we all must pass in order to be entrusted with immortal life. The beautiful part of this is, we do not have to do this alone.

His divine power has given us everything we need for a godly life through our knowledge of Him who has called us by His own glory and goodness ~2 Peter 1:3[26]

What we must understand about God is that, while God was forming our "innermost being," God was equipping us with His knowledge, His glory, and His goodness. At the moment of conception, we have all that we need through God's divine power! We have all that we need as we pass from being the seed of God, created by God, to the seed of man, born in the image and likeness of God through man and woman! This is where the journey begins. I know that as some of you read these words, you are wrestling with your childhood, and the parental choice that God made, by which to give you life. While I can't answer why God made your particular parental selection, I do know that God is, well, God. His thoughts are not our thoughts, and His ways are not our ways! What I can answer with most assurance, is that God knew exactly what was necessary to create you. Maybe, just maybe, it was necessary for you to be born into the family for which you were born, because that was the only DNA recipe that would create the uniqueness of you! Do you think that it was worth it? Maybe you cannot understand it now. Maybe you cannot see the benefits now. However, when you align yourself on the journey of the heart, and you begin to walk this journey of predestination manifestation, you will catch a glimpse of God's earthly plan and purpose for your life! The more intimate you become with God, the deeper God will take you as He reveals His hidden plan. God may even give you a slight glimpse of His eternal plan for your life! How amazing to walk with God, the founder and creator of all things, while God talks to you, while God shows you the end, and how that end resulted in your beginning. God delights in showing us His will. God loves to commune with us and reveal Himself to us. "The steps of a good man/woman are ordered by the Lord; and He delighteth in his way." (Psalm 37:23)[27] I also like the NLT translation of their same verse, which states the following, "The Lord directs the godly. He delights in every detail of their lives." Knowing that God is there to order our steps on this journey, and furthermore, He desires to delight in us ... Is that not the definition of intimacy, a walk of synergy between God and humanity that God orders our steps, and He delights in our ways? We will discuss more about that later in this chapter, but here, I want you to fully conceptualize that God desires to walk this journey with us, and to direct our paths, if we would only allow Him.

Hit Replay. What will your spiritual DVD say? An Introspective Monologue

---

There is no greater agony than bearing an untold story inside of you −Dr. Maya Angelou

---

As we sit and ponder, in an attempt to evaluate the thematic preludes of our lives, we are led into a spiraling replay of a series of events that have shaped the life and course of our very existence. We find ourselves on a trip down the long lane of memories past, so vivid that our physical response mirrors the very response of long ago. In the moment, of recall, we dialectically engage in weighing the pros and the cons, trying to exercise the use of the precisioned hindsight to correct mistakes, forgetting that time passed cannot be changed. When we awaken from the subconscious trip, and reality's sting begins to grip us back into consciousness, we realize we were gone for quite some time. Exploring time passed, as if there was something to gain, other than pleasurable memories, we so tightly cling to the pain. So intent on not only reviving but expressing our feelings and hurt, that we forget to assert our truth, and our worth.

If I asked you to hit play on the spiritual DVD of your life, what would your walk, your talk, and your character say? Would it speak that I am broken, beaten, and abused; and that despite the differing opportunities, I still refuse to choose to embrace the many blessings God has for me, refusing to forgive and press through the pain that has claimed my destiny? Will your DVD say that people-pleasing is the way I make decisions and live my life? And, if others are not happy, than neither am I. Are you able to describe the very essence and embodiment of I; or is the you, that God created, too closely mimicking others' lives? When I call your name, does your individuality stand and greet me at the door? Or does the mask of your thousand faces show, again, and engage me just once more? I find it a shame, that time and time again, you neglect your unique self and desire to be someone else.

If you pressed play for me, what, then, will I see? Can I smile and say, "I truly got to meet thee?" Are you consistently consistent, or are you a roller-coaster of emotions, so much so that your truth is non existent? Can you explain to me, the YOU I am supposed to see? Can you please refrain from any anger at my frustration? You get angered at my frustration, my irritation, and agitation, when I purpose to seek separation from your constant emotional fluctuation. The truth is, that I just do not desire to be a part of your continual negativity and emotional uncertainty.

I know that each of us has a story deep inside; and sometimes the truth seems so ugly that it is better to hide. Yes, you are hiding that truth, so that others cannot see that truth is mangled in the darkest and worst aspects of thee.

That's the masking we do when we are in a different setting, afraid and scanning the crowd to see if we can guess what others are thinking. That mindset, is flawed and inherently evil, it must be rejected, and those thoughts fully extinguished. Know that your pain is your story, and in that story, there is Glory! There was a lesson to learn that will propel you and teach others not to worry. The difference between a saint and a sinner, they say, is one loves self enough to brush himself off and continue on the way; while the other one stays and wallows in the pain of time present and past. The shackles of that pain sucks life from the very soul, and the sinner lost from grace remains, until one day in the mirror, while looking, they notice that they are gray and old.

Rejected by Man, Chosen by God: Image Crisis

OFTEN TIMES, AFTER we have received the re-filling from God during the season of waiting, we step into our next season only to face additional obstacles. One obstacle that I have often struggled with, which is called the, "bait of Satan" by John Bevere[28], is offense that occurs because of rejection. Whether it is actual rejection, or simply our ruminating, self-defeating thoughts that creates subliminal catastrophes out of minor disagreements or criticisms, feelings of rejection can be hard to overcome. We can recite multiple scriptures to ourselves in hopes that this conscious and unconscious repetition will quell the stabbing pain in the pit of our soul, or stop the consistent replay of hurtful situations in our heads. However, I have found that exploration and surrender are the keys to overcoming feelings of rejection from others.

Exploring entails asking ourselves questions such as:

What is this person saying?

How am I perceiving this relational interaction?

Why does what was said, or done, feel so conflictual or painful?

What does this relational interaction say about me?

Therein lies a discerning introspection that can, through the work of the Holy Spirit, reveal to us the true impetus of the feelings of rejection. As humans, we are masters at the subliminal, interactive exchange called transference and countertransference. We are creatures of association, meaning that we attribute similar thoughts and feelings onto people, places, and/or things that are similar. Our behavioral responses are triggered by our perception of stimuli. Stimuli perception happens at the speed of thought, as our interactions are sifted through years of pain, happiness, weaknesses, trauma, highs and lows, words spoken, and non-conditional interactions, as they are being interpreted for our deciphering. If we are not consciously aware and whole from the various systemic interactions and their impact on our authentic self, we decipher what is being communicated from a skewed perspective.

It takes a mind transformed to be able to discern the truth, and it is from that truth that we can then form an accurate interpretation of self and others. It is from an authentic core that we form a healthy self perception that moves us past feelings of hurt, pain, and rejection, to a place of wholeness; not denying our experiences, but understanding that they are just that, experiences. "Experiences" has a historical connotation, and the mere fact that you can think on experiences, is proof that you have been able to move beyond those trying moments physically. But, what about mentally and emotionally?

I am who God says I am! Who I am is based on God's word, not my experiences! Perceptions can be deceiving; even my own perceptions of me.

---

1 Samuel 16: 6-13 states that "when they came, he looked on Eliab and thought, 'Surely the Lord's anointed is before him.' But the Lord said to Samuel, 'Do not look on his appearance or on the height of his stature, because I have rejected him. For the Lord sees not as man sees: man looks on the outward appearance, but the Lord looks on the heart.' Then Jesse called Abinadab and made him pass before Samuel. And he said, 'Neither has the Lord chosen this one.' Then Jesse made Shammah pass by. And he said, 'Neither has the Lord chosen this one.' And Jesse made seven of his sons pass before Samuel. And Samuel said to Jesse, 'The Lord has not chosen these.' Then Samuel said to Jesse, 'Are all your sons here?' And he said, 'There remains yet the youngest, but behold, he is keeping the sheep.' And Samuel said to Jesse, 'Send and get him, for we will not sit down till he comes here.' And he sent and brought him in. Now he was ruddy and had beautiful eyes and was handsome. And the Lord said, 'Arise, anoint him, for this is he.' Then Samuel took the horn of oil and anointed him in the midst of his brothers. And the Spirit of the Lord rushed upon David from that day forward. And Samuel rose up and went to Ramah."[29]

As I reflect on the story of David and Samuel, I'm reminded of the obedience that rested in Samuel when God led him to anoint the new leader. I am reminded that who God chooses, sometimes man rejects. Man tends to look at the outside, qualifications, credentials, who knows who, and the like. Not Samuel! You see, when he visited Jesse's sons in order that God might select the next king, Samuel would have chosen every son but David, because of worldly standards. This is seen in verses 6-7, *"When they came, he looked on Eliab and thought, 'Surely the Lord's anointed is before him.' But the Lord said to Samuel, 'Do not look on his appearance or on the height of his stature, because I have rejected him. For the Lord sees not as man sees: man looks on the outward appearance, but the Lord looks on the heart.'"*[30] However, in his private submission to God's will and not his own, David was the one chosen, because that was whom God selected!

Relationships often taint our ability to use discernment and remain committed to the obedience that is required for God's purpose to manifest. One can only fathom what would have happened if Samuel would have allowed, both, his intellect and friendships to make the decision regarding the next king. How would the course of life have changed if Samuel selected what God rejected? What changes are orchestrated when you fail to maintain your level of obedience to God's will? What happens when you choose what God has rejected? What happens when you choose to focus on man's rejection instead of God's acceptance.

There are times in life when decisions are made that are contrary to what has been prophetically spoken to us. In these moments, we must maintain our faith in what God has spoken, and not what man deems acceptable. The enemy is clever in disguising situations, circumstances, people, places, and things, to mimic the dream God has implanted on the inside of you. You must remember that if it does not look like what God has spoken, let it go! Why? It is not real! It is only a clever distraction; it is but a shiny object that mimics a coin, only to later be found to be a piece of trash. If you would take but a moment to shine the light on those things that are presented to you in this life, God will reveal the origin and authenticity of the matter and, if its a person God will reveal the condition of their heart.

Therefore take to heart that God is faithful! What he has promised concerning you will manifest in the way God promises, at the time God desires, and, it will exceed all expectations. We must place our focus on the acceptance of God, and not be consumed with the opinions and feeble worldly expectations. God often chooses what man rejects and thus we must remember to walk in utter obedience despite the rejection from those closest to us. We must be brave and courageous in embracing our authenticity even when it looks foreign to those around us. Obedience on the journey of the heart is key. The blessing and prosperity of another is directly connected to your obedience. Your obedience is not simply about you, and it's impacts are not just for "you." There are many who are attached to what manifests to and through your obedience; and you will be held responsible for your decisions. While God is a God of grace and mercy, God, yet, has expectations of you; and if you do not meet those expectations, chastisement is the result. God needs you to abandon the rejection and become who he has designed for you to be; nothing more and nothing less. Therefore, my dear brothers and sisters, be not dismayed because all things will work together for good concerning YOU. Isaiah 41:10 states, *"Don't be afraid, for I am with you. Don't be discouraged, for I am your God. I will strengthen you and help you. I will hold you up with my victorious right hand."*[31]

Why so many questions?

WHY IS IT that we expect God to be our instant magician? Granting every prayer that we have ever uttered or whispered? When God does not respond in the way that we want, we doubt all that God has ever done or God's response. But then we let our mouths confess an untruth, positing that we truly trust God. Trust requires assurance, even in the dark, that though one may stumble, one will never fall. Trust requires that when God speaks, we will forsake all; and that nothing else in life supersedes obedience when God calls. Shall we not chase God the way God has chased us? Shall we not forsake all the ways God forsook all for us? Shall we not spend countless nights crying out of disappointment over God, the way God so diligently bottles our tears inside heavenly glass jars? Shall we not want God's will, the way we profess that we do? Do we truly believe God desires what's best for me and you? Shall we pursue God's will the way we pursue earthly treasures, emotional leisures, positions of power, and spotlight of being the center of man's attention and applause? Have we become that shallow and precarious in our concept of self that we feel worthless when we are not co-signed by the acceptance of man? Who made man to rule over man; and why is there more preparation and diligence placed into altering to man's demands? When we can separate our worth from humanity and place it where it truly belongs, in the Hands of the Great I Am, we become something supernatural, something out of the this world ... literally.

Check your Voice

BEFORE WE CAN become dedicated and committed to the journey of the heart, we must know God's voice and evaluate our voice. In this section, we will explore our voice. Sure our voice is what we hear on the outside, however, our inner voice is the determinant that has the power to control our decisions. It is through our inner voice, mimicking the voice of God, that we can find the answer to all of the questions that plague our mind.

Jim Loehr notes in his work, *The Power of Story*, that we each have a private voice. This voice is a part of the story that surrounds the foundation of who we are and who we will become. This private voice is attached to our values and beliefs, which, then, develops the prism by which we see the world.[32] This private voice has powerful regulatory and creative power. This private voice, along with it's themes and messages, impact beliefs, emotional responses, behaviors, and habits that form our character. On this journey, we must examine, not only our inner voice, but the external voices that sometimes become our inner voice. Take a moment to think. Whose voice rings loudly in your ear and has a transitory impact on your life? Whose opinions and expectations have you allowed to shape your decisions and choices on this journey? What are the messages that you repeat to yourself in the valley and on the mountain top? Do these messages echo the trauma of the past, reverberate messages of rejection and pain, or do they align with scripture and what God has to say about you?

We must replace worldly voices without the voice of the shepherd. Jesus shares with His disciples and shares with us today through the Holy Scriptures, "My sheep listen to my voice, and I know them and they follow me (John 10:27)."[33] He also states, "to them the doorkeeper opens, and the sheep hear his voice; and he calls his own sheep by name and leads them out. And when he brings out his own sheep, he goes before them; and the sheep follow him, for they know his voice. Yet, they will by no means follow a stranger for they do not know the voice of the strangers (John 10:3)."[34] What Jesus is asserting in this dialogue with the disciples, is that the sheep should not only know the voice of the shepherd or leader, but this should be the only voice they answer to and follow. Any strangers, meaning anything contrary to the voice of God, anything contrary to the word of God, should be refused, abandoned, neglected, or discontinued. The message to us on this heart centered journey, is to isolate all of the voices that are NOT the shepherd, and purposely abandon those voices. Then, hearken under the voice of the shepherd through scriptural study, prayer, and meditation; replacing all other voices including your own internal voice, with the voice of God. Jeremiah 10:23 states, "O Lord, I know the way of man is not in himself; it is not in man who walks to direct his own steps."[35] Jeremiah has learned on his journey, that God's voice and direction are indispensable, and without it we should expect to be lost. God's voice is essential for life, and His voice must usurp in importance and intensity, any other voice that attempts to utter guidance in your life. If you listen to God's voice, and God's voice supercedes your private voice, then you can build your life and the storyline of your life on a new foundation. A foundation of truth. A new life. A new story.

New Story:

WE MUST NOT be afraid of abandoning the expectations of others, and the foundation created on sinking sand, to rebuild on a divine foundation with God's opinion at the center. In fact, God's opinion is all that is required. When God created humanity, the Ish and Ishshah, no other opinion was needed. No other creation had any input into the design and characteristics of man. No other creation was consulted when God designed the purpose of His creation; therefore, this solidifies the importance of consulting God and God alone. Once your foundation is stabilized and reinforced, then you can begin to, through divine intervention, draw others of like spirit, who help to sharpen the iron in your life.

We cannot flourish and maintain a healthy life when unhealthy voices have input into who we are and who we become. The truth is, I am fearfully and wonderfully made. I was created with purpose and equipped with all that I need to achieve success, happiness, joy, pleasure, and peace in life. The world did not tell me this, my creator did. The truth is, I was created to lead others to a place of healing, because this brings me the greatest pleasure. We are all called to be a place of refuge, to be a voice of hope, and to show others the healing power of God through self. This is my soul's purpose. What is yours? The truth is, I love to travel and am restored when I am in nature getting a glimpse of God's creative power. The truth is, I am closer to God when I am in a place of rest, and peace. The truth is I am a great mother, wife, friend, pastor, therapist, mentor; and if I ever feel like I am lacking in an area, I have only to make my request known unto God. This story is my story; and it takes me to where I want to go. It is grounded in reality, and it stimulates hope in me, hope in those around me, and hope for my future goals. I am assured that life is short, but I was created for pleasure, joy, fellowship, ministry, and ultimately to reflect God and His glory on earth, so that others make it into eternity. When I am assured in who God has created me to be, it grants me permission to develop and imbue an attitude of "yes." It frees me to be all that God has intended for me to be, which means I can serve as a model for all that I meet. This is my story ... what is your story?

The Attitude of "Yes" on the Journey

WILKINSON, IN HIS text, *You Were Born for This*[36], talks about the master key and the power of saying "yes" to God. He asserts that we only want to say yes to God, when it looks like, sounds like, and feels like our will and anything contrary to that, elicits an unwavering "no." However, to say yes to God is freedom. To say yes to God is to yield to the will of Almighty God. Saying yes to God, and yes to ourselves, will allow us to walk into an unknown territory. It will allow us entry to the new life that the Holy scriptures say that we can have in Christ. It allows us to experience some things never experienced before. Trusting in God unlocks doors to our inner purpose, our inner destiny, our pre-destined design, and a feeling of fulfillment and peace that we have never felt before. Alignment and synergizing with God takes us to a place where miracles are possible, and unlocks the revelation needed for true discipleship.

Jesus said, "Greater works shall you do than this,"[37] and this is revealed when we are operating in the full power of Almighty God.

Saying yes to God gives us a spirit of boldness. Saying yes to God gives us a spirit of diligence. Diligence means to exhaust every possibility, to consistently and persistently search for that which is needed; it is to achieve a state of untiring, unremitting exploration. Diligence is an INtentional quest to find what God has for us. Diligence creates an insatiable quest to cross over into the realm of assiduous and sedulous inquisition. To hunt and scour for the sine qua non. To reach a state of mental, emotional, and spiritual deprivation, understanding that we are indigent without the One. As we thirst for drink and hunger for food, there should lie within, this ravenous desire for God. Should our craving not be holistically met? We must stand, ever searching, with an unrelenting diligence as we seek God. Diligence is the behavioral expression of our yes.

My Inner Voice: A Monologue

I HAVE FOUND, in this life, that we seek God with the most diligence when we are in a place where our complacency has left; when we have everything we could possibly want and more, and yet, we still feel as if we are on an exhaustive search for something unknown. We spend our lives in search of money, fame, fortune, relationships, careers, and education, all in an attempt to acquire and feel what only God can give. In my nostalgia, I have found myself in a distant time that makes me ever grateful for moments with God. However, in my melancholy, I feel that only half of me has received the nourishment that is necessary for survival. I crave God like air; like water on a squelching hot summer day. From the deepest depths of my being, I want to scream in wanton ask for something, anything, until I realize that in all of my restlessness, both mental and physical, that I don't know for what I must ask. I can only send a request that I need you Lord. Where do I go in these moments where what I desire is as dark as night with no stars in the sky? Where do I turn when the paved path of my past is clearer than the path of the future and its tasks?

Then, my prayer sings like the psalmist as I chant, Lord, I've almost achieved all of my life goals! I try to live an obedient life each day. I have more than I could ever ask for, yet, I feel like I'm complaining because I desire more. But, wait ... this desire does not stem from me; it stems from within my soul that is closely aligned with thee. Is this you, are you talking from the depths? Recognizing my inner voice at this moment just seems foreign to me. I'm losing grips with the epicenter of this being I thought was me, but it appears that she has transformed from mediocrity to authenticity. She's connected to the one who is her voice. The one who has decided that she no longer has a choice. The one to whom the entire world hearkens at the Voice. God has decided that because of her diligence, God would respond to her call, but it is up to her to remember to trust God's truth, even when it doesn't resemble her expectations at all.

Diligence is effort unlike I've ever experienced before.

Diligence is like running a marathon to which you do not know where it would end. The anticipation coupled with the exhaustion creates an intense feeling of anxiety and excitement that is strong enough to make one crawl out of one's skin. It is so immensely tremulous that your body cannot create the serotonin required to calm. Your mind will consistently ruminate. Searching with all precision; and no matter how hard you seek, you still cannot conceptualize what you are looking for. It is like craving something you have never tasted before. It's wanderlust, without a destination. It's a craving with an unknown satiation? It's having a question with no answer. Why? Because the answer to all that we seek is God. The satiation to all cravings, is God! The ultimate dose of serotonin that will ease the most complicatedly plagued of minds is God! The destination that we so desperately seek, is God.

It's sometimes easier to remain in a bubble of willful ignorance, than to have a touch of mindful expanse. It's easier to travel down the road of past, than to trust and walk into your future. It's easier to live below your expected purpose than to rise and walk into your destiny. Life can be confusing and impossible to navigate alone. And, yet, with everyone around you, there will be days that you still feel that daily, you travel alone. There are days when you will lay in dismay, because you think you have lost your way. Some days you will sit in stillness paralyzed by the unknowing of what lies next. However if in those moments, you will diligently seek God, God will hear. When you diligently seek God, God sees you! When you diligently chase after God, God leads you! If you are relentless in your search, God believes you! God believes that you will follow only God's leading. God believes that you will only follow God's teachings! God believes you will not sell out to this worlds false riches, and no matter where you go, you will take God with you. Diligence and persistence birth the existence of, not only this worlds riches, but favorable existence with both God and man, and by the touch of God's hand, you will rule every land, to which there is a touch from your feet or your hands.

So seek God-! Seek the Lord and the Lord's strength. Diligently seek Adonai's face continually (1st Chronicles 16:11),[38] because the Lord has looked down from heaven upon the sons of men to see if there are any who understand, who seek after God (Psalm 14:2).[39] Without faith, it is impossible to please God; and all who come to God must believe that God is, and that God is a rewarder of those who DILIGENTLY seek Him (Heb 11:6).[40] Isaiah said it best in chapter 55 and verses 6-7, "We must seek the Lord while He may be found, call upon God while God is near. Let the wicked forsake his way and the unrighteousness his thoughts; And let him return to the Lord. For the Lord loves those who love the Lord and the Lord promises that those who 'diligently seek me will find me.'"[41]

How do we exhaustively seek God with all diligence?

1. Start with God daily.
    i. Make God your first thought; rise early, simply to seek God.
    ii. Let worship of God be your first word.
    iii. Intently listen for God early in the morning.
2. Praying without ceasing.
    i. In everything, consider God.
    ii. Listening and meditating is also a form of prayer.
    iii. Make sure to listen twice as much as you speak.
    iv. Forsake the busyness of the day, and find quiet time to align with God and dream.
3. Inquire of God, God's will for your life.
    i. In everything, consult God. From your daily attire, to your eating habits, work agenda, and parenting practices, make God the epicenter of all of your decisions.

The Choice: Will you Choose God or the World?

As WE SEEK to increase our understanding of our own heart-centered journey, we must realize that our birth into humanity ushers us into a dilemma; we have choice. What is choice? The Merriam-Webster Dictionary defines choice as the existence of two possibilities with the power of selection. From a theological context, this is referred to as "free will."[42] Did you know that you have the power to make a choice? You can choose God, or you can choose this world. God entrusted you with the power of free will, and even when our first parents chose mortality and worldly treasures, God, yet and still, designed a plan for our propitiation so that we, you and I, can continue to exercise our free will -our choice. God could have, at the very moment our first parents sinned in the garden, removed our freedom of choice. God could have instituted an eternal cessation of our free will at that very moment; and He still maintains this prerogative, yet, God allows us the free will of choice, hoping and desiring that we, His creation, will choose Him.

Before you can understand your journey, you must first examine your choice. Probe the inner-most aspects of yourself and all that is around you. Have you forsaken all others and chosen God? Or have you become so indoctrinated in the miraged apparitions of this world, that you have made an unconscious choice, preferring the prince of the power of the air? It is imperative that you thoroughly inspect your choice, because this choice impacts your journey to include your final destination. I know some of you are asking, "how can I determine which choice I have made?" I believe there are two areas to which we can focus to gauge our choice: time and money. Ask yourself:

What or whom occupies most of your time?

Where are your finances spent?

I believe time and treasure, to include our finances and assets, provide a holistic picture of where your heart is. In fact, Luke 12:34 and Matthew 6:21 both state the same principle. *"For where your treasure is, there will your heart be also."*[43]

Let's look at this a bit deeper. Jesus said in Matthew 19:21, "If you would be perfect, go, sell what you possess and give to the poor, and you will have treasure in heaven; and come, follow me."(ESV)[44].

1 Timothy 6: 17-19 states, "As for the rich in this present age, charge them not to be haughty, nor to set their hopes on the uncertainty of riches, but on God, who richly provides us with everything to enjoy. They are to do good, to be rich in good works, to be generous and ready to share, thus storing up treasure for themselves as a good foundation for the future, so that they may take hold of that which is truly life." (ESV)[45]

What is Jesus saying? What is the principle here that we must learn? To be successful on this journey of the heart, we must "seek first the kingdom of God, and His righteousness, and all these things shall be added unto you." (Matthew 6:33)[46] If God is not the motive, reason, or the centrality of all that you are and all that you do, maybe, just maybe, your choice is not what you think it is. I'm not saying that you cannot buy the shoes and the purse. I'm asking you to examine why you are buying the shoes and the purse. If you are purchasing the shoes and the purse as a reward because you have been an appropriate steward of God's resources, you can view this as a blessing from God, or what we term the "added unto you." However, if you are purchasing these items to fit into the world's standards of "keeping up with the Joneses," then your focus is on the world and conforming to the precepts and standards of this world. You cannot serve God and have your eyes and mind fixed on conforming with this fallen world. I encourage you to fix your eyes upon Jesus. Hebrews 12:1-2 states, "Therefore, since we are surrounded by such a great cloud of witnesses, let us throw off every encumbrance and the sin that so easily entangles, and let us run with endurance the race set out for us. Let us fix our eyes on Jesus, the pioneer and perfecter of our faith."[47] Jesus knows the path, for Jesus' word is clear. "I am the way, the truth, and the life. No one comes to the Father except through Him."[48] Jesus has the keys to unlock your purpose and the roadmap to your destiny. You must, however, make Him your choice. The choice is yours!

In AD 500, Augustine in his work Confessions, posed a question that each of us must ask ourselves. The question posed was "How can you draw close to God, when you are far from your own self? Augustine prayerful response, "Grant, Lord, that I may know myself that I may know thee."[49] This too should be our response.

If you desire to know yourself and God, you must be diligent and deliberate about seeking Him. That is what makes your journey, a journey of the heart. It's no longer a life in response to the external, but a life lived because of the internal. You are the temple of God, and your heart is where you encounter communion with God. In order to complete this journey, you must encounter God and this encounter requires your whole heart.

Prayer of Transformation:

Lord, help me to be still before you. Lead me to a greater vision of who you are, and in so doing, may I see myself—the good, the bad, and the ugly. Grant me the courage to follow you, to be faithful, to become the unique person you have created me to be. I ask you for the Holy Spirit's power to not copy another person's life or journey. God, submerge me in the darkness of your love, that the consciousness of my false, everyday self falls away from [me] like a soiled garment.

In Jesus' name, amen. (Peter Scazzero, 2014)[50]

Chapter 4:
THE ENCOUNTER: IAM

You give attention to the smallest matters, my suspicious doubts, and to the greatest. You know my coins are counterfeit, but you accept them anyway, my impudence, and my pretending! – Rumi[51]

I Am

I AM IS to embody the fullness of you. It means to embrace your God-ordained design, unapologetically. Wherever you are, wherever you desire to be, you arrive with the essence that only you can carry; because it's yours and yours alone. You understand, holistically, that you are and always have been Plan A. You must own it, walk in it, and exude it from every pore of your being, You are S.H.E. Spiritually and Holistically Enough. Why? Because you understand the power of I AM, the power of being, and the power of the one true and Almighty God that lives on the inside of you. Everywhere you go, you know that you do not arrive alone. You arrive with a divine companion; one that requires the most sophisticated of appearances, the most honorable of character, leaving behind the most memorable of encounters. Everyone you entertain should feel, without a shadow of a doubt, that, they, through you, have been in the presence of Almighty God.

Maybe no one has ever told you, but you are authentic. There is only one bonafide and genuine version of Y.O.U. More importantly, you are necessary. There is no one in the 7,530,103,737 (according to the latest world count) that can assume the role and possess the gifts and purpose divinely revealed in you. Real and veracious, you step on the scene with supernatural power fueled by the internal dwelling of the Holy Spirit. The seed within you shines a light so bright that it cannot be dimmed; it seeps from your pores and makes you swell, a bright beam of light. This light of God, on the inside of you, cannot be dimmed; and anyone who attempts to quench your shine will not be spared from shame.

The divine essence of you lives within, but if it is not visible above the surface, it is because your soul has not been cultivated. In order to boldly embrace the I AM, you must first become heart centered. Why? From the heart, flows the issues of you. Knowing self, and embarking on the journey of you, requires patience, commitment, dedication, and self-love. The heart is demanded for self-development. It is on this jaunt, and I say jaunt, because the word of God tells us that life is like a vapor that appears for a little while and then vanishes away (John 4:14b), that we must devote immeasurable time getting to know ourselves. We cannot truly know self until we know God, for it is knowing God that God begins to reveal the predestination plan for you. No one, absolutely no one, knows this level of insight and foundational information about you, except God. For who knows us better than the one who created us? It was God who concocted the very gestation of your being, brewing you in the deepest chasms of His being, birthing you forth in His protection, and for His purpose. It is on this journey that you must detect all foreign ideas, concepts, and beliefs that do not align with the spoken word of God in your heart, so that you can actively and purposefully abandon all the falsity that has been supplanted into your being by others. You must abandon all that is contrary to what God has spoken and ordained, and regain a focus on truth, committing to its journey, seeking significance, purpose, and authenticity in God and God alone.

I AM is prophetic and revelatory. I AM is bold and free. I AM is gifted and talented. I AM is a dreamer and innovator. I AM is discipline and order. I AM is controlled and obedient. I AM is holy and peculiar. I AM is pleasing to God because SHE/HE is living purpose. I AM is PREDESTINATION MANIFESTATION. I AM confirms commitment.

When we say "I am," we give our word, in faith, that we will do, we will be, or we will become that to which we have pledged. We are co-signing that we will never abandon the mission and the journey despite the trials that may arise. We assert that we know the destination, and we are bold and brave enough to travel this journey because we have a relationship with God. Even if we don't know all the stops on the map while we travel the journey, we know the destination, because instead of beginning with the end in mind, we chose to begin with God in mind. This God-first mentality allows us to be privy to some of the intimate details, the deep and hidden things of God such as red flags, road signs, and stops that we will make along this heart centered journey; because this is essential for navigation and ensuring that we remain on the right track. Even when we are lost for a second, God always gives us away of escape that guides us back onto the correct path.

God spoke to Moses through the burning bush with a response of, I AM that I AM. Meaning I am God; I AM inexhaustibly me. I AM, because there is no other like me. I will not compare myself to anything else in creation, because there is none like me. Therefore, my response yet remains, and this response is also my name … I AM.

Only an encounter with God can reveal I AM.

The Blueprint of Y.O.U.

BEFORE WE ARE born, manifest in the flesh, there is a blueprint for our lives. There is a unique design for us; in fact, this design is so unique that there is not another like it found on earth. The diversity of humanity is a representation of the diversity of purpose. Your blueprint belongs to only you. The only fingerprint that will open the door to what belongs to you is yours! This is why we cannot become jealous or envious of the assignments, assets, or the elevation of others, because what God has assigned to you and for you, cannot be given to another. We must learn to have faith that our God created diversity and uniqueness for a purpose. We must understand fully that work embedded in the design of you.

You must begin to understand and walk in the purpose for which you were called. You do a great disservice to the world trying to determine your own purpose, and abandoning the God's mission for your life.

Do you desire God's will in your life more than you desire your own? Are your expectations aligned with His? Do you even know the doors, opportunities, and assignments that will only be accessible when your fingerprint is scanned? During a ministry training several years ago, I posed three questions to a group of 20 individuals, and the responses were quite daunting, but expressively representative of the condition of man at this present time.

> Question #1: What is your spiritual gift?
> Question #2: What is your purpose?
> Question #3: Are you walking in your purpose?

Of the 20 individuals present, only 2 individuals raised their hands. Two of the 20. That is only 10%. Of the individuals in the room, at least 15 were well into their 50's, 60's, and some in their 70-80's, and yet, they were not able to identify their spiritual gift, nor the purpose for which they were created. How can one truly live without knowing the blueprint for our lives? How do we live from day to day without desiring to know whether there is more for us, or whether there was more for us to do? This highlighted the deficit in both ministry, and individual relationship building with Christ. We are wandering blindly without a roadmap. This beacons an encounter with God.

Who am I that you are mindful of me?

Psalm 8:3-6
When I consider Your heavens, the work of Your fingers, the moon and the stars, which you have ordained. What is man that You are mindful of him, and the son of man that You visit him? For You have made him a little lower than the angels, and You crowned him with glory and honor. You have made him to have dominion over the words of Your hands.' You have put all things under his feet. [52]

As I meditate on the omnipotent, omniscience, and omnipresent holiness of our God, I often wonder why God desired to create me.

The options of the infinite are just that ... infinite. Yet, you God took the time to fashion me with specification, definition, description and enumeration that has no comparison except for Thee. I often wonder, with all of Your Divine prerogatives, and all of my sin stained inclinations, why did you not just keep me with you or allow me to remain a permanent fixture of your inner most thoughts? Yet, you allowed me the opportunity to encounter you, and the results of the encounter was ... me ... created in your image.

"What is the body? That shadow of a shadow of your love, that somehow contains the ENTIRE universe." –Rumi[53]

In His Image

"And God said, Let US make man in our Image."

IN A WORLD of disarray, of confusion, longing and searching ... In a world where everyone is seeking acceptance from one another, or as you would call them, people pleasers ... In a world where being FAKE is the NEW NORM, and where drug use is so rampant because people are afraid of reality ... In a world where one in five individuals suffer from some form of mental health disorder, whether it be depression, anxiety, schizophrenia, or bipolar disorder ... In a time when every time you turn on your TV screen, someone is being injured or killed ... What better time than now to reflect, redirect, and refocus on who we really are, the power we possess, the internal ability to declare and decree, to walk in faith with the expectation? A time to examine ourselves and realize that we are MADE IN GOD'S IMAGE.

As we examine Genesis 1:26-27, we see our God defining the divine blueprint of humanity and setting the date for mankind's encounter with Him. "Then God said, 'let us make mankind in our image, in our likeness so that they may rule over the fish of the sea and the birds in the sky, over the livestock and all the wild animals and over all the creatures that move along the ground.' So God created mankind in His own image. In the image of God he created them. Male and female, He created them."[54] God created us to be His family. God's unchanging plan has always been to adopt us into His family by bringing us to himself through Jesus Christ.

Our very first encounter is with God. Our daily first encounter should be God, but is it?

As you awake in the morning and look in the mirror, what is it that you see? What do you really see? Do you see fault? Do you see shame? Do you see regrets? Or do you see beauty, love, discipline, faithfulness, unity, humility, and sacrifice? Do you see Jesus? Do you even know what Jesus looks like? With what the world has become, is it still easy to see Jesus? Are you assisting the cause; and, in that, I mean, are you showing others what being Christ-like looks like? Or, are you blending into the mold that this world has shaped and formed? Are you one of them? Or are you a part of Him?

In the encounter, God reveals who He is and who You are! Only the creator can reveal the essence of the created. In this chapter, it is my goal to lead you into a practice of daily encountering God. This will require personal reflection, or what we call in the clinical world, "introspection." Introspection cues an individual to search deep within themselves, to examine who they really are, their motives and their actions, to soul search, honestly. It requires removal of the veil with accurate self-examination so one can uncover who they are and decipher if the life lived is being lived authentically. This spiritual contemplation will reveal the frequency and intimacy of the encounter. The encounter will reveal if you are the Imago Dei.

Imago Dei: Image of God

Now, just so no one gets lost, we are going to examine the word, "image," for just a moment. The Hebrew root of the Latin phrase for "image of God"—*imago Dei*—means image, shadow or likeness of God. You are a snapshot or facsimile of God. At the very least, this means humans occupy a higher place in the created order because we, alone, are imprinted with God-like characteristics. We are different because God created us differently than any other creature that walketh this earth. God breathed His breath, His soul, and His spirit into you. This is the essence of the encounter. God's breath made you different. God's breath made you unique. Your godlikeness is the path to your greatest fulfillment. You will feel the greatest pleasure and wholeness when who God made you to be is fully developed and expressed. It is God's intent that you are to represent Him on this earth, to mirror His image wherever you are; because you are created with His very nature and His DNA.

Theologians have long debated humanity's synonymity with God, but the answer becomes clear when we study the attributes of God. If we could take a snapshot of God. What would we see, and what would it reveal about humanity created in God's image? Is there similitude between the Creator and the created? The answer is yes! If you have encountered God, it will be evident in every area of your life. There is glaring parallelism and harmony between God and us! So, just as when someone shares how you much look like your mom, or act like your dad, we are now going to examine how we look like God.

> 1. **I AM CREATIVE**. We are creative, because God is creative. Look around you. Do you see all the differences in people in the world? Look at your neighbor, and then, look at yourself in your mirror. The sheer power of creativity. Every human makes things. God has gifted us with the power to be innovative and creative. God has embedded into us a dream

that can become reality. The artist creates by painting the fire in her soul, the musical composer creates harmony with just a few notes, and every time we speak, we too create a reality for ourselves and others. Every human has the capacity to make things, to create, because we are all made in the image of a creative God.

2. **I CAN COMMUNICATE.** You communicate because God communicates. Our communicative and creative God SPOKE everything into existence, and he imbued this same attribute onto us. The human ability to think and reason, to use language, symbols and art, far surpasses the abilities of any of the other created beings. This gift was bestowed upon us, when our communicative God's image was imprinted on us.

3. **I AM RELATIONAL.** Being relational is all about our interaction and interconnectedness with something or someone outside of ourselves. The very essence of God is relational, and this essential quality has also been imprinted on humanity. You are relational, because God is relational. When God spoke "let us make man in our image, in our likeness" and "it is not good for man to be alone," (Genesis 1:26, Genesis 2:18)[55] God was revealing the "us-ness" in the very nature of God, and the "us-ness" that is intended to exist upon His creation. The capacity for a relationship with God extends to humans, which is why the Genesis story declares that God created Eve for Adam because, "it is not good for man to be alone." So for all of you who think you can make

it on your own, just know that is not in God's design for mankind. We are made for unity, bonding, and love.

4. **I AM INTELLIGENT**. You are intelligent, because God is intelligent. Logical, sequential thought flows from the orderliness of God's mind. As a result, we are all intellectuals. We each possess a mind and a way of thinking and learning and because, God's intelligent image is imprinted on our lives, we possess different kinds of intelligence. It is however, up to each of us to continue to develop our mental capacities to their fullest. How can we do this? By studying God's word so that we can grow spiritually. We must move from that shallow soil in which the roots can't grow, to a place of increased spiritual wholeness and perfection in God. Study of God and His word will stimulate and expand your mind beyond the limits of this world. This is why He commands us not to be conformed to this world but to be transformed at the seat of our intellect, because what the mind can conceive, reality can achieve.

5. **I AM WISE.** God has given humanity all the knowledge that is needed to live a life of joy, peace, and prosperity. God has even given humanity access to all the keys to Heaven, as well as, the keys to a joyous life on this side. Use the gift. Use the knowledge. Study His word, because it is all that we need to gain wisdom.

6. **I AM HONEST**. God always represents things as they really are. Numbers 23:19 states "God is not human, that

He should lie, not a human being that He should change His mind. Does He speak and then not act? Does He promise and not fulfill?"[56] All of God's knowledge and words are true and the final standard of truth. God encourages each of us to remain truthful at all costs, for we know that whatever is true, whatever is noble, whatever is right, whatever is pure, whatever is lovely, whatever is admirable, if anything, is excellent or praiseworthy, think about such things. (Philippians 4:8)"[57]

7. **I AM FAITHFUL.** God will always do what He has said and fulfill what He has promised. We, too, must walk in faithfulness with one another, seeking to always assist and minister to the needs of another, despite their transgressions against us. This trait of faithfulness is a virtue instilled in your DNA, it is always accessible, but we must access it and make it a part of not only our dormant internal being, but prioritize it as a quality of external excellence.

8. **I AM FORGIVING AND MERCIFUL.** We can go on and on about our forgiving God. The blood of Jesus has cleaned every stain of iniquity; if only we should repent and forgive our brothers and sisters when they have done wrong or harm to us. Forgiveness is required for heavenly entry and if you fail to forgive, then you will not be forgiven. It is just that simple!

9. **I HAVE SELF CONTROL.** We all feel emotions, because God feels emotions. Many times, it is referenced in the bible, God's anger, wrath, pleasure, and the varying emotions that

we feel as humans. These emotions emanate from the character of God and are now an inheritance to us. But, despite emotional responsiveness, God always maintains self-control. Thanks be to God. We sin daily and frequently offend the Holy Spirit. If God lacked self-control we would all be doomed to Hell. However, because of God's mercy and self control, we are able to repent and be redeemed. We may fall down but we are able to get back up again.

10. **I AM LOVE.** God is freely and eternally giving of himself for the good of others. Are you reflecting love? Do you really love your neighbor as you love yourself? Or, are you continually condemning them because they don't live up to your standards? Let me share this with you. God wants us to love real people, not ideal people. So, each time you run into that rude boss, or the bossy little lady that never smiles that sits on the second row of your church pews, intend to pass the test by dispensing love. True love is unconditional.

11. **I AM BEAUTIFUL.** God is the sum of all desirable qualities, which is the definition of beauty. The indivdual and unique differences that you have are the qualities that makes you unique in the eyes of God. God didn't create ugly, ratchet, fat, flawed, or no good. God created YOU! Everything about you, from the mole on your nose, to the crooked little toe. Everything about you is made in God's image. So, when you disrespect yourself, use self-defeating thoughts, engage in name calling and gossiping, slander and belittling, you are offending God, because everyone, and I

mean, EVERYONE is made in His image. Sure we might not agree with how someone acts, or how someone talks, or maybe even how someone dresses. But, the way to change incorrect behaviors is to model the appropriate behaviors. How can someone recognize a behavior change is needed unless they have some good to compare it to? After all, Jesus had to come to earth to exemplify to us how to live. So, now, it is our task to let our light shine and model Christ-like characteristics to the world.

To be fully human is to fully reflect God's creative, spiritual, intelligent, communicative, relational, moral and purposeful capacities, and to do so holistically and synergistically. In God's infinite creativity, there are no duplicates. You are the only you there has ever been, or ever will be. And, because you are an ambassador for Him, you are called to represent your heavenly Father in the earthly realm. You are to re-present him, or present him, again and again and again in every avenue of both the spiritual and secular arena. You are to be the encounter in this world. It should be said that when people have an encounter with us, they have had an encounter with the spirit of God, who lives within us. The world has formed this erroneous and limited concept of God and you are called to demonstrate His greatness in your lifestyle. God has called you to **BE HIS SHOWCASE**, and everything about you should reflect the glories of the kingdom, from the clothes you wear to the way you talk. Everything that speaks to your station and quality of life should all demonstrate the limitless glories of the kingdom of God.

You are alive because God wanted to create you. He deliberately chose your ethnicity, the color of your skin, your hair, and every other feature. He custom made your body, He determined your natural talents, your spiritual gifts, and the uniqueness of your personality. He planned the days of your life in advance and chose the exact time of your birth and death. God left no detail to chance. Nothing in your life is a mistake, nothing is arbitrary, it is all for a purpose. You are custom made with the exact specifications needed to be uniquely you. God's motive for creating you was love, and He poured out His all, forming your very substance. God was thinking of you before He made the world. In fact, you are why He created it. You are the focus of His love and the most valuable of His creation. You were made to express God's love.

Character after the ENCOUNTER

OUR OUTER BEHAVIOR is representative of our inward man. Behavior comes as a result of processing thought. There is no behavior that occurs that has not been thought through, for this is the way that God created us. The mind is the control center of behavior. That's why the scripture is says that they will know a tree by its fruit. Fruit is an outward product of inward cultivation. Fruit is an outward manifestation of the heart, mind, and spirit's focus and desire. The Spirit conveys what Christ bestows. Christ imparted His life and power to us through the Spirit. This means, that because we are now unified with Christ, the Spirit now begins to speak to us on the inside. As the Spirit speaks to us on the inside, and our thinking, our desires, and our mindset begins to shift, God begins to bestow some things on the OUTSIDE, which is proof of the encounter.

Why this topic of discussion? Because, there are many who say they do not know how to live the way God called us to live. After the encounter, we must learn to live as the new creature, created in Christ. In the preceding section, we looked at the eleven "IAM's" and in this section, we are going to look to the Paulian epistles to determine some additional God-like criterion. We learn how to live like God by studying the character and nature of God. We are without excuse because we have examples to follow. The apostle Paul provides a thorough analysis of what we should look like as Christ emulators and what does not look like Christ. In Colossians 3, Paul provides an inspired detailed analysis of character after the encounter. Since we are spiritual temples created for the indwelling of the Spirit of God, there are practical implications for how we as believers must live our lives. Now that you are new men and women in Christ, says the apostle, live like new men and women. You have said goodbye to your old life; and have done away with all those things that were characteristic of it. You have died with Christ, now it is time to act, speak, and think anew, so as to make plain that Christ's "death" is not a mere figure of speech, but a real event which has severed the links which bound you to the dominion of sin.

There is a true follower of Christ, which is quite different from the "self-professed Christian." The life of the follower consists of the renunciation of all sinful propensities and pursuits so that the new nature, divinely implanted within, may find outward expression as fruit.

In contrast to the *I AM* proclamations previously mentioned, here are some *I AM NOTs*:

As followers of Christ, we should not engage in or take OFF:

   a. Fornication
   b. Uncleanness
   c. Inordinate affection
   d. Evil desire
   e. Covetousness
   f. Anger
   g. Wrath
   h. Malice
   i. Slander
   j. Obscene Talk
   k. Lying

And some attributes we should put ON:

   a. Compassionate hearts
   b. Kindness
   c. Humility
   d. Meekness
   e. Patience-bearing with one another
   f. Forgiveness
   g. Love
   h. Thankfulness

The encounter changes who we are. We, holistically, become a new creation, and can follow Jesus all while leading others to His transformative power. After the encounter, we must forsake all and follow Christ. As we follow His footprints in the sand, we become translated into the divine image that we are created to be.

The Encounter births a new you ... Embrace your authenticity. —Sha'Leda Mirra

---

Chapter 5:
LEARNING HOW TO DWELL

Naked:

I walk naked with you, Lord. Bare, stripped naked. Fully exposed in my natural state.
 Why? Because I Trust You.
 Why? Because I Need You.
 Why? Because you are the supplier of my every need.

I walk naked with you, Lord. Bare, stripped naked. Fully exposed in my natural state.
 Why? Because of your unconditional love.
 Why? Because you accept my flaws.

Why? Because you accept me for me, and what change is needed, you create that change in me.

I walk naked with you, Lord. Bare, stripped naked. Fully exposed in my natural state.
Why? Because you delight in seeing the unmasked, uncovered essence of me.
Why? Because you complete me.
Why? Because when I am undressed, you purpose to clothe me—uniquely, flawlessly, in unequivocal beauty.
I just want to be accepted by you Lord, simply be who you created me to be.
I just want to radiate the light of your rays and shine in the spotlight of your beauty.
I just want to be accepted by you, Lord; and allowed to grow into my true form. And, I know that if I am bare with you, you will mold me, and make me, and I'll be transformed and never conformed.

You are the potter, I am the clay. Mold me to be like you, Lord: striving to walk in your footsteps, and walking in the shadow of your ways.
I don't want to hide behind make-up, Lord; branded clothes and cultural norms.
So, that when I look in the mirror, my greatest desire and pleasure is to see your smile, your delight in what You have formed.

So, I walk naked with you, Lord. Bare, stripped naked. Fully exposed in my natural state.
Knowing you find pleasure in the one who is bare for you, who delights in you—because that woman, you will praise!

How comfortable are you with Exposure:

If I passed around a make-up remover cloth asked you right now, to remove your make-up and sit here amongst the members in the audience, how comfortable would you be?

Bare, fully exposed for all of the flaws in your face to see?

Would your mind be flooded with thoughts and perceptions of others' conceptions because of all that others can see?

Would you be distracted, and require the redirection of your self-perception, because all that you have tried so hard to cover up, mask, or perpetrate, if you will, is out there for everyone to see?

If I gave you a perpetrator remover cloth, and asked you right now to remove the mask that has covered your soul, and expose it for all to see,

Bare, fully exposed for all of the flaws in your soul to see.

Would your mind be flooded with thoughts and perceptions of others' conceptions because of all that others can see?

Would you be distracted, and require the redirection of your self-perception, because all that you have tried so hard to cover up, mask, or perpetrate if you will, is out there for everyone to see?

I ask again, If I gave you a perpetrator remover cloth, and asked you right now to remove the mask that has covered your soul, and expose it for all to see? Would you reflect the fruit of the spirit, would you expose contently—with composure—or would you become indignant with me?

So when, if at any point, are you truly bare?

So when, if at any point, are you comfortable with your authentic self?

Do you know her, have you seen her, where did she go?
Asks your inner soul.

She ran away, she's pretending, she is brand-new. Can you help me find her? God gave us work to do. Men, this same dialogue applies to you too.

Let his word permeate your mind, let it examine your motives. Let it test your resolve, and let it introduce change from within.

The Wait

I'm reminded of Juanita Bynum's song, *"I Don't Mind Waiting."* In this song, she notes that, "there are times in life when situations are going to occur, where you may look to the left or to the right and you can't find any answers there is no one, anywhere to help you." Maybe it is a midnight hour, maybe you are in a place alone, and no matter how loud you yell, there is no one that can rescue you or heal the pain that you feel. It is in those moments of desperation and isolation that we are reminded of Isaiah 40:31 which reminds us, *"they that wait upon the Lord, shall renew their strength; they shall mount up with wings as eagles; they shall run and not be weary; and they shall walk and not faint."*[58]

This scripture is one that is recited most, when we are in valley experiences, when all around us has changed, and when we are in a physical, mental, and emotional state of unfamiliarity. When all that we have known and worked hard for has seemingly disappeared. We find ourselves standing in a foreign land, with no clear vision, nor desire, to step toward the recovery of our destiny. This was once me. However, one of the greatest lessons learned is that we must expect unfamiliarity on an unfamiliar journey. Though we may feel lost, with God's presence and His leading, we are never lost. God is always leading and reality is, new is always unfamiliar.

There is something about a valley experience, because it is in the valley that we find that we need God more than we ever needed Him before. Purging and pruning for godly character development happens in the valley called, WAIT. Someone wise once asked the questions:

How can you know God is a healer, if you've never been sick?

How do you know God is a provider, if you have never been in a state of need?

How do you know that God is a deliverer, if you have never been in a trap?

How do you know God is a way maker, if you have never been LOST?

And even in our circumstance, though we may cry out incessantly to Him, sometimes His answer is to simply *wait*. In this popcorn generation, "wait" is synonymous with denial, "no," and "you're not good enough." In our flesh, the wait is hard, UNCOMFORTABLE, UNCERTAIN AND CONFUSING. In the wait, we feel a loss of control, we become indecisive, we become irritable and sometimes bitter and angry. We are tossed to and fro because, since the moment in the garden, when we tasted the forbidden fruit, we have been on this quest of knowledge. We have an incessant need to walk the journey of life with a road map, expecting active dictation of the path we will take, and the answer to every "why" question that develops along the way. As humans, and especially God's chosen people, we become lost when the way is not plain, or when the manna or the provision is not constant. We simply don't like to wait. I must admit, the wait is difficult, especially when the enemy is dangling all of the different options to take in front of you. Any path looks and feels right, when you think you are lost!

There are some BENEFITS AND REWARDS that are attached to the wait.

There are some blessings and promises of God that are increased and intensified in the wait. A perspective change, and a renewed alignment happens in the wait! There are some life lessons that provide the ladder to the new season, in the "wait." If only we knew on whom we were waiting ... My God!

The Lesson of the Eagle:

ANCIENT HEBREW CULTURE revered eagles as mighty warriors. A majestic bird, having tremendous eyesight with a visual acuity six times better than that of humans. They are capable of seeing over 1-1/2 miles away. This exceptional vision, along with their long, sharp talons, make them very effective predators; known for being strong, calculated in their actions, bold, beautiful, graceful, long life, with a spirit of independence, and they are loyal, courageous in dangerous, turbulent weather, soaring above storm clouds and to safety. They care fiercely for their young, and are a monogamous, faithful bird; they stay with the same mate their entire life. If either bird happens to die, the eagle will find a new mate. But, despite how majestic and equipped these birds are, they still find themselves in a state of intense challenge and trial.

Legend says that an eagle, at the age of around 30, flies to a high place in preparation to endure a harsh trial of endurance and change. It can't fly because its feathers are overgrown. Therefore, it plucks all the feathers from its body. It plucks its talons from its feet because the talons have grown curled and useless. Its beak has grown too long and curled. It breaks its beak against a rock. Defenseless, it cries out and waits for the time of renewal. Other eagles hear its cry, and come to aid. They fly overhead, scaring off predators, and they bring food to their incapacitated friend. God provides for the eagle in the "wait."

In the wait, we may feel lost, abandoned, useless, vulnerable, not on top of our game. We may feel last instead of first, insecure, neglected, and if we allow the feelings to fester, it can lead to more serious issues, such as, depression and anxiety. We must know that while the wait is hard, God always makes sure that while we are waiting, while we are in this vulnerable state, He will send his ministering angels to us. Friendships will strengthen, all of your needs will be supplied, you will be protected and nourished, while in the valley of WAIT.

Just like with the eagle, we go through trials of endurance and change. This is necessary to shape our Christian character and faith. In such a time, I encourage you to stand still. We may not be able to physically change the circumstance, but God's word is clear, in that while we are waiting on the answers, while we are in the stagnant valleys of life, if we keep our minds on God, we will soar mentally, spiritually, and emotionally above life's storms, because God will keep us in perfect peace. There is a promise of renewed strength and courage to overcome obstacles if we WAIT with faith, trusting in the Lord's sovereign timing.

To wait for the Lord for strength, implies that we recognize that we can not save ourselves. To wait upon the Lord for strength, implies that we recognize our weakness. We recognize our misery outside of Christ. We intentionally place our hope in the origin of ALL.

Waiting on the Lord necessitates two key elements: a complete dependence on God, and a willingness to allow Him to decide the route of the journey, the stops along the way, and the ultimate destination. We must sit in the driver's seat, next to the Divine, who knows our heart and knows the plan. We must yield to trusting God with the timing of events, because His timing is perfect. We must not be afraid of pausing or waiting on instruction, even while remaining in the present circumstance. We must know, with all certitude, that the wait is seasonal, and it, too, will pass. In the wait, we must exercise a purposeful and expectant focus on God.

The wait is an INtentional choice to be actively still and quiet in our hearts, listening for His voice and watching for His intervention. The wait is not for events to work out as we want, but rather for God's will to be done. The very situation that you are facing right now could be a trial of endurance and spiritual stamina, but if the message of the eagle is not enough, the text goes on to describe another truth, when it says "those who run shall not be weary, and they that walk shall not faint (Isaiah 40:31)."[59] This defines the very essence of fortitude. In what appears to be physical stagnation, God is increasing fortitude, revelation, and perseverance that will prevent us from growing weary and fainting. So, the text is teaching us that we ought to seek our strength from God. The wisdom within these holy scriptures serves to revitalize us as we face the day to day battles that every child of God runs up against. With strength from God, we can face the peer pressures of the world. With God's strength, you can do anything *but* fail.

While we wait, we must, "Be still, and know that HE is God." We must posture ourselves to wait with patience, wait calmly, and wait with expectation. Why is this posture important? Because hurry is the death of prayer and interrupts the intimate connection between the creator and the created. Dallas Willard describes hurry as "the great enemy of souls in our day." He further states "being busy is mostly a condition of our outer world; it is having many things to do. Being hurried is a problem of the soul. It's being so preoccupied with myself and what myself has to do that I am no longer able to be fully present with God and fully present with you. There is no way a soul can thrive when it is hurried."[60] Inner calm creates the intercom to God. In other words, it makes the connection. Not only does God hear you, but you hear him. God speaks to people who take the time to listen. You must want to hear from God, and this is demonstrated when we withdraw to a quiet place, away from distractions, so that can be fully present with God. We must wait expectantly, fully focused on God. God is watching you to see if you're ready to receive His word. When you wait calmly and patiently in expectation of his answer, you then experience His blessed assurance.

I remember a practical example that happened between myself and my youngest daughter. I walked by my youngest daughter, Chrystian. She was sitting at the door, fully dressed, hair done, and she had her new baby doll, just sitting there peering out the sliding glass door. I called her name to gain her attention and I said, "Baby, what are you doing?" She replied, "I'm just waiting." You see, her grandmom has promised to come by and pick her up and take her to Walmart, and she was waiting.

This is how God desires that we WAIT on HIM.

She was sitting at the door waiting quietly; and had I not walked by, I would not have seen her at the door waiting. She was quiet and calm.

She was sitting at the door patiently. She wasn't nagging me, saying "Mommy, Mommy, Mommy! Can you call my Nana to see when she is coming?"

She was waiting at the door with great expectation. How do I know this? She was fully dressed, doll in hand, perched so that as soon as she heard her Nana's voice, she would run and go with her. She wanted nothing else, but to go with her Nana. And, there was no convincing her that her Nana was not going to keep her word!

So remember the promise is SURE.

How sure is that promise? Well, consider that this promise is made by the almighty Creator of the heavens and the earth, the One who sustains all things,
the One who has created us with all our idiosyncracies and complexities.
The same One who has created the physical universe.
The same One that created man and woman.
The same One who sustains life in His creation.
The same One who bore calvary's cross for our sins.
Is He strong enough to strengthen us spiritually? Of course, He is. He's the creator.
He's the sustainer. And, He has given us a promise.
All those who wait upon the Lord, SHALL RENEW THEIR STRENGTH. THEY WILL MOUNT UP ON WINGS AS EAGLES. THEY WILL RUN AND NOT BE WEARY. THEY WILL WALK AND NOT FAINT.

That's God's promise for you.

Is There Anything Too Hard For God?

WE GO THROUGH life with a sense of urgency that often prompts us to detour from the ordained course that God has established for us. Prioritizing our own will above God's will, we work to make things happen, birth clones of dreams and visions that God has given us as a tool to help guide us along this journey called life.

I call them clones, because they are not the authentic version of the promise. Once you begin opening the package of this "gift" or "blessing," as you say, with much affinity, yet, with a vain attempt to give God credit for something that you truly and intrinsically know did not originate within Him, you realize that all is not what it seems. You wanted it right now when God said wait. Then, a spirit of bitterness and resentment sets in, because what appeared to be a shiny diamond in the rough, what you thought was the manifestation of a dream and vision that God showed you in the most vivid detail, was only a shiny piece of glass. A broken particle. A remnant of what someone else enjoyed, and now serves as their trash.

Sometimes, we can become so focused on the promise, that we miss the path. The path is the route that we must take in order to encounter all that is required for the promise to birth forth. We miss the path, because it is only revealed through the divine revelation of God, and can only be seen with a supernatural eye. Our forefather, Solomon, built the ancient temple from the vision and specifications revealed through a blueprint that only the supernatural eye can see. It took Solomon years to complete the temple and his royal palace. (1 King 9:10)[61] For 20 years, Solomon followed the path and the blueprint of Almighty God. What is most interesting, however, is that this same blueprint, passed down to him from his father, David, who was originally ordained to build the temple. But, because of the sin stained blood on his hands, and because he detoured from the path that God laid out for him, David was not able to fulfill the assignment that God had for his life. Have you ever detoured from the path of God after God has revealed the blueprint? Will God have to commission your seed to do a work that was originally assigned for you? Despite our shortcomings, God's plans will be established. Research asserts that the site on which the temple was built was sanctified thousands of years before it saw completion during the reign of Solomon. The land that was selected and sanctified for the building of the temple, which was a threshing floor, was actually associated with Mt. Moriah, which is the same location that Abraham brought his son Isaac to sacrifice to the Lord. We know that God offered a substitute in place of Isaac, but this foundation, was selected even during the time of Abraham, and embedded in the heavenly blueprint for the temple that would not see it's walls constructed until thousands of years later. Talk about an intentional God.

Anything worthy takes time to manifest so we must learn how to dwell.

Let's look at the story of Abram and Sarai, better known as, Abraham and Sarah to gain more insight supporting the importance of the wait. Abraham was 75 years old when God spoke to him and gave him the edict, commission, and the promise of Genesis 12.

> "I will make thee a great nation.
> I will bless thee, and make thy name great.
> Thou shall be a blessing.
> I will bless them that bless thee.
> I will curse them that curse thee.
> And in thee, all families of the earth shall be blessed."[62]

God later revealed the promise of a seed to Abram; for how can you make a great nation without offspring from your loins? The second time that God spoke to Abram concerning his seed was in Chapter 13, after the separation of Abram and his family from Lot and his family. Though it took many years to manifest, and many mistakes (Ishmael) in the process, God, yet, delivered on His promise. God's word never fails. We, however, must learn how to patiently dwell.

And so Isaac was born.

It is amazing how God continues to remind us of the vision and the promise, so that we will not forget that God, who began a good work in us, will see it through to completion until the day of our Lord Jesus Christ. This timing may not look like our timing. God is not bound by time, nor space, nor any of the physical constraints that easily beset us. What appears to be years in our perception, is only moments to God. Since God is not bound my time, His promises to us are not bound by time. Back to Abraham. God continued to remind Abraham, that despite his old age and the physical, biological, and emotional frailties of life, God was still able and would keep His promises. When we believe the Lord, as Abraham did in Genesis 15:6, despite what our circumstances may look like, despite what the doctor may say, and despite what the scholars proclaim, it will be counted to us as righteousness, as it was counted unto Abraham.

Because God is ... God!

Ecclesiastes 3:1-8, states, "there is a time for everything, and a season for every activity under the heavens."[63] This time and season is appointed by God and aligned with His perfect will. We must seek to synergize ourselves with God's perfect will, agenda, and timing, or else, we risk being out of sync. When we are out of sync, our perception of time is skewed. We begin thinking using our mortal knowledge versus the divine providence of an All-Knowing Omniscient God. We forsake a life of obedience and trust, for a will of our own that provides no answer and no remedy for that which we seek. Our will cannot make manifest the providence of God, no matter how closely the clone may resemble the original. We must rest in the word of God. We must trust in the word of God, knowing that it is God who began the work, and it is God who will see it through to completion, if we would just wait on him. Is there anything too hard for our God? Maybe you have thought your situation was too much for God to handle. Maybe you have allowed the mountains in your life to skew your vision of the Great I AM. Maybe, you have forsaken the path of God with all of its valuable lessons and preparatory practices, and chosen your will instead. Whatever the issue, know that God is able to do EXCEEDINGLY above all that we can ever ask or imagine. So, simply trust and dwell in God and when someone asks you the question, "is there anything too hard for God?" let this be your response ... Absolutely NOT.

Surely the arm of the Lord is not too short to save, nor His ear too dull to hear. -Is. 59:1[64]

Learning How to Dwell

WHEN MOSES SET out on this journey from Egypt to the promised land, he had no idea that it would take 40 years to get to the divine destination. He had no idea that these same people he sacrificed his life to deliver, would be the reason he did not reach his destination. During the commission for the journey, Moses engaged in a long debate with God about his lack of qualifications to deliver God's people. In my sanctified mind, I believe Moses didn't want to go and deliver God's obstinate, stiff necks, whining people ... But, because He loved the Lord, He went anyway.

When we set out on a journey called life, we, too, have no idea of the twists and turns that will meet us. We have no idea what we will have to overcome on the wilderness road. We have no idea of the disappointment, heartaches, and heartbreak that will meet us as we travel the journey of the heart toward destiny. Many trials and tribulations happened during these 40 years. In fact, the intended 40 day journey was extended due to the obstinance and complaining of the people. God had just shown himself faithful and delivered them. He answered the prayer of ancestors stemming back to generations before Moses was even born. Now, rescued from deliverance, and on the journey to the promise, they began to lose hope and because things were not going their way, they threatened to turn back to the captivity they were just miraculously delivered from. This demonstrates the mentality and mindset of humanity. We are all guilty of questioning God's divine prominence when it surpasses our limited insight and understanding. Yet, we say we have faith. Faith, howbeit, cannot exist in what is seen. That is called sight. Faith is the substance or building particles of our hopes and invisible evidence that is deemed visible because of who God is. Our desires only manifest when they are aligned with God's desires. Trusting God should be all the evidence we need to believe. He who kept Moses faithful to the journey, is the same One who will keep us faithful, as long as we learn how to dwell.

Moses believed while he walked the journey, and so should we.

And, yet, God remains faithful to His word.

We must be careful. Unlike Moses, we must not allow the Korah's in our midst to lead us to a place of anger and confusion, which, then, moves us out of the will of God. If you do not know who Korah is, Korah, along with 250 other Israelite men, rose up against Moses after his return from Mt. Sinai with the commandments of God. Every opportunity Moses was absent, Korah was plotting and scheming to hinder the journey by discrediting Moses. However, when you are anointed and appointed of God, He will consume your enemies; and guess what happened ... God opened up the earth in Numbers, chapter 16, and swallowed not only Korah, but all those that were "too close" to him. God swallowed all those who sought to thwart God's divine plans, making His point poignant … CHOOSE THIS DAY WHOM YOU WILL SERVE.

And Job said "I know that you can do all things and no plans of yours can be thwarted" –Job 42:2[65]

Moses, like us today, had to be reminded that no matter what is going on around us today, if we would just escape and get to God and dwell in the secret place of the most high, we shall abide under the shadow of the Almighty God. What does it mean to dwell in the secret place?

To dwell means REMAIN hidden under the covering of Almighty God. The place where His shadow is your defense and protection; where, when others see you, they see the Great I AM. To dwell means to live, to be settled in, to lodge, to stay. It requires residence for a length of time. It is not a visitation, it is not an abode of convenience, it is a place of rest and refreshing for, both, you and God. I implore you, don't wait until you get in the wilderness; begin to dwell with God NOW. So, when the wilderness experience comes, you will be prepared and ready for battle.

When you choose to dwell in the secret place, and you abide under the shadow of the Almighty, God becomes:

> Your fortress and refuge.
> A place you can go and be free from life's trials and tribulations.

A place of retreat for refreshing.

A place free from disappointment, heartache, and betrayal.

A place of protection.

A place of privilege, as God allows you behind the veil.

What are the benefits of dwelling in the secret place? You will live fearlessly! You are able to dwell because you understand, with blessed assurance, that a thousand may fall at your side and ten thousand at your right hand, but **NONE** shall not come nigh. Because, you have made the Lord your refuge and your habitation, no evil shall befall you. No plague shall come near you or anything that belongs to, or is connected with you. Why? Because the Lord shall give his angels charge over you to keep you in all your ways. These angels, they are going to keep you safe, propped up and protected. It doesn't stop there. The Lord states, because we love Him, because we know His name and have a relationship with him, He will set us up on High; He will grant us stewardship over the works of His hands. The Lord says, when we call upon Him, He will answer.

There is no better place to be than in the dwelling place with the Great I AM. When we learn how to dwell, the seasons and transitions of life will only serve to bring us closer to the One, and have no power to distract, nor destroy.

So don't fear. God is on the journey with you; even when the seasons change.

The Seasons of Life

RECENTLY, I HAVE heard a plethora of gospel songs proclaiming that it is a season of blessings, a season of favor, and a season of prosperity. As a child, I remember playing some old records that my mom acquired from a friend, and in those records was the most beautiful gospel music I have heard to date. I recall hearing this song by an unknown singer with the following lyrics:

> *There is a time for everything, and there is a season.*
> *God has planned everything, and He has a reason.*
> *A time to laugh and a time to cry, a time to be born and a time to die.*
> *There is a time for everything, everything.*

Her voice still resonates in my spirit.

SO, AS I reminisce to the most innocent and yet confusing moments of my life, I can't help but replay a series of events strung together with some connection, some semblance to each other. Some of the historical events were pleasant, such as friendships developed, meeting my husband, having my daughters, and finishing my college degrees. However, in looking at the pleasant memories, I am reminded of the eventful and painful events of my past; those that taught me lessons that, though in the moment, seemed unfair, they were pivotal and assisted in the molding and reshaping of who I am now-a new person in Christ. As I replayed these thoughts in my head, I gained a clearer picture and a thorough understanding of what a "season" actually is. Sure, we know that seasons refer to four particular times of year that are characterized by weather changes and a prodigy that even shortens or lengthens available daylight hours. Each season is distinct, characteristic of certain phenomena, and has both it's positive and negative aspects. We immediately think of the 15 degree weather of winter that kills all of the plant life and shrubbery in our yards, or the 110 degree heat of summer that, we, Floridians experience that keeps us indoors instead of enjoying the outdoors. But, there is much more to understand about the word *season*, as applied to our inner self, as it speaks to major markers and life altering experiences in one's life. Each season has benefits, and lessons to be learned.

Each season, seasons us!

JUST AS THE word of God admonishes us to pay attention to the seasons of nature so we can prepare for the coming change, so, too, shall we observe the seasons in our lives, in order to prepare for change and learn the necessary elements for promotion and elevation. There is a time of separation, for the preparation, that is needed for future elevation. So, the questions I am posing to each of you today are: What season are you in? What do you see, taste, feel, and smell that informs your discernment of this season?

Let's spend a moment to ruminating about the season of separation and preparation, and the resultant elevation. As I kneeled in prayer, God poured these words into my spirit:

A Monologue with God. God spoke, I listened.

You are in a season of preparation. You have been foretold to learn of, and pay particular attention to what is going on around you, in this season! The lessons are necessary for where I am taking you! They are necessary for equipping. Nothing happens by happenstance; you must walk separated, you must walk in the spirit so that you can behold the great and marvelous things I have in store for you! Watch as you walk. Some lessons are hard because every season has its toils and snares, but if you trust in me, I will use all things for your GOOD! I am the orchestrator of life. I am He who makes the wind blow and the tree to produce the oxygen needed for the survival of man. I am; and she who abides in me will not only prosper, but flourish, far surpassing those of mediocre stance. From your bosom shall flow that which you never thought achievable. Making your dreams look minuscule in comparison to my plans for you. From your bosom, you shall birth a revival, a resurgence of my people reminding them of who I am, and why they are my people in the first place. Each season has its' lessons, learn them. Teach them.

A season, God said, is necessitated by the equipping, beginning, first, with separation, which has its focal epicenter on building a closer relationship with me. Then, revelation is granted, the divine ability to see with eyes in the spiritual realm, a path that is not observable by the human naked eye. God says, I AM He who causes the mountains to form and the sky to produce rain! I AM He, who thought of, ordered, and created this world and all that you see in it! Am I not more than capable of creating a life for you that touches and revives every sense in your body, bringing glowing pleasure and delight? Bringing overflow so magnificent that you are lost in amazement, and know this level of provision only comes from I? Am I not the God of your forefathers, the one

> *who preordained you from the foundation of the world; who fashioned the very texture of your skin and the very cusp of your lip? Am I not He that sets angelic protection and girds your loins when the enemy mounts? Am I not He that sets you on the wings of an eagle, so that the precision with which you see and the viewpoint from which you discern is supernatural? I am HE! I never change. From season to season, I AM is always the same. So I implore you, observe this season, discern this season, feel the season, smell this season, recognize this season, collect pebbles in this season, grow in this season, be in this season. In every season, watch with me! Observe with me, listen with me, recollect with me! Write with me, partake with me! You will be ever so thankful when you cast your eyes on your history and find nuggets of knowledge that are beneficial to you.*
>
> *-God*

So, I say to each of you, in every season, watch, listen, recollect, write, partake, enjoy, be silent, laugh, touch, smell, visualize, become mesmerized, be deliberate, be purposed, be free. Why? Because, even on the dreary and rainy days, like today, there is a benefit and something to learn. God is always teaching. Are you listening?

What season is it on the outside? What season is it on the inside? Pay attention, learn the lessons, be ye separated, invest in purposed preparation, and I promise, your elevation will exceed your expectation!

Then, you will have learned how to dwell.

Chapter 6:
MY DAILY WALK WITH INTENTION

My Daily Walk with Intention

This is the beginning of a new day.
I can waste it or use it for good.
What I do today is important because I am exchanging a day of my life for it.
When tomorrow comes, this day will be gone forever, leaving in its place, something I have traded for it.
I want it to be a gain, not a loss;
good, not evil;
success, not failure.
In order that I shall not regret the price I paid for it today.

-Author Unknown

Intention

We have often heard it said that, you see the glory, but you do not know my story. Well, today, I challenge you to tell. Can you tell me? Tell a tale of the rudimentary intentionality it took for the fruit of your tree to bear all, fully exposed for the world to see. The morphing from the caterpillar of old, to the beautifully arrayed butterfly. Have you reached a destination that showeth forth the radiance of your fruit, or the coat of many colors that allows you to stand out from the crowd of mediocrity and commonality? Or are you still there, standing, pretending, like the cursed Fig Tree of Matthew 21:21? Beyond the leaves of your outer garments and raiments, can we see the fruitfulness from your life? Are you still searching for meaning, or do you feel you have arrived?

Intentionality is a word that is often used, but less often understood. We throw this word around haphazardly, highlighting our lack of understanding when our lives are juxtaposed with what we profess. For we know that intentional and haphazard are antonyms, or do we? Just as we misuse the word intentional, we also fail to apply it to our daily lives. We fail to plan, we fail to order our days, and we take pride in coloquisims such as, "it is what it is" or "you only live once." Slogans such as these, feed the negative cognitive messages and beliefs buried deep within our subconscious mind such as, "I have no control over life," "I am not disciplined," and, "I can't do anything about it." Thoughts such as these, promote a victim mentality, contributing to a lack of effective problem solving and decreased motivation for change or transformation. So let's take a look at this word, "intentional," for just a moment, so that we can truly uncover what this word means and understand it's practical applicability.

According to Dictionary.com, *intentional*[56] means the following:

Done with one's own will; Voluntary; Done with awareness of an end to be achieved; or a readiness or eagerness to accede to.

Now, let's take a moment to examine what intentional is *not*. Below are some antonyms for the word intentional:

Accidental.
Chanced,
Haphazard.
Random.
Compulsory.
Casual.
Extemporaneous.
Impromptu.

When comparing the definition to the antonyms, we see a notable difference. Now, compare these words, both, the definition and the antonyms, to your life. Which ones describe you? Are you the deliberate, conscious planner who has purposed intent each day? Or are you the autopilot who lives based on luck or chance, randomly making decisions and providing extemporaneous remarks that you later regret? When we lack intention, we lack direction. The truth is, when we lack awareness and purpose, we are simply lost. We mismanage everything, including time. It's not about 'having' time. It's about making time. If it matters, you will make time. I found myself remembering all of the times I responded with the excuse, "I just don't have time," when, in fact, it was not about time, but the mismanagement of the time I had. Peter Drucker notes, "until we can manage time, we can manage nothing else."[67] When we fail to live intentionally, we fail at many things to include time management, order, discipline, and adequate planning.

Life is about intentionality. Everything ever created was created intentionally, on purpose, and with a goal in mind. The conception of life, the earth, the separation of light from darkness, the waters from the land, the animals, and even mankind, were all created by an intentional God. We can look back to the beginning of creation and see this exemplified in Genesis 1. We can also see intention, through the countless other biblical examples such as, the anointing of King David, the birth of Jesus, the death of Jesus, and the redemption plan for man. The reason that King Solomon posits that there is nothing new under the sun, is that God not only preordained life and existence, God also knew through the power of foresight what was going to happen, and thus God prepared a plan for that. It was with calculated intention, decision, and precision along with willful preparation, and invested commitment, that God created; and keeps us, leading us to our final destination.

So, why then do we lack intentionality in our lives? Were we created to be random, compulsory beings who live on a whim, conditioned to "go with the flow?" Well, in order to answer this question, one can go back to the book of Genesis and find our creator, God, intentionally creating all things. Each day, had its own purposeful agenda met. Whether it was creating light and separating it from darkness or creating man from the dust of the earth, no actions performed by God were unintentional, casual, or impromptu. We were all created with deliberate intention. We are no accident. From the strands of hair on our heads, to the chuckle in our laughter, God created each of us with intentional specificity. So, what does that say to us? We should pray as David prayed. "Lord teach us to number our days that we may gain a heart of wisdom." (Psalm 90:12 NIV)[68] We must understand that life is but a vapor, and that we must treasure each day by living on purpose.

There is power in intention. Intention is, that which is done purposely and deliberately. It is what is conceived and birthed, when we have not only thought through, but also planned for every possible scenario, expecting an outcome and counting the costs. It is calculated, intended, planned, studied, and premeditated. But, what's more, is that intention requires commitment. When we set an intention, understanding the costs and the benefits, we know and understand that this thing that we have birthed, requires our unwavering and unyielding devotion. Despite the hardships, let downs and disappointments, we must remember, we set this intention!

Before God created man, before God created you and I, God counted the costs. God, also, remains committed to us, despite our daily shortcomings, despite our frailty, pride, and self-seeking ideologies. You were INTENTIONALLY created, knowing that there are times when you will make mistakes, lie, cheat, steal, and commit all sorts of evil. God could have destroyed us, as God did the fig tree long ago, but God's faithfulness to us and God's commitment to the intention, demonstrates God's love, because God cannot lie. Jeremiah 1: 4-5 (ESV) reads, "The word of the Lord came to me saying, 'Before I formed you in the womb, I knew you; Before you were born I sanctified you; I ordained you as a prophet to the nations.'"[69] God intentionally predestines us, so it is imperative that we align with God, asking Him to number our days so that we may know the frailty and limited time we have for the mission.

Paul told the Ephesians in Chapter 5:15-17 (ESV), "Look carefully then how you walk. Live purposefully and worthily, and accurately, not as the unwise and witless, but as wise, sensible, intelligent people, making the very most of your time, buying up each opportunity because the days are evil."[70] In other words, he admonished them to live on purpose, not carelessly, but making every minute count. Intentionality, according to Dr. Cindy Trimm in her book, *The 40 Day Soul Fast: Your Journey to Authentic Living*, notes that order and intention give you clarity of thought and greater control of your time.[71] This means that we must eliminate time wasters such as gossip, social media, television, internet surfing, and the like, unless there is an intention behind the use of them. Sure, surfing the internet can be beneficial for research; however, it is a time waster when used as a method of procrastination. Intentionality allows us to examine not only what we are doing, but why we are doing it, and what is there to be gained in the action. During this process of examination, we can then eliminate those things that are not beneficial or purposive, and replace them with actions that are fruitful and bring honor and pleasure to our lives.

Kirk Byron Jones, in his book, *Holy Play: The Joyful Adventure of Unleashing your Divine Purpose*, notes, "The best we can offer one another comes from our own authenticity and creativity. Authenticity and creativity is birthed by intentional living."[72] In closing, I will leave you with this Proverb: "Consider well the path of your feet and let all of your ways be established and ordered aright." (Proverbs 4:26, NIV)[73]

An intentional life is a fruitful life. Allow the order and balance of God to show as your fruit daily, by being intentional in every way! Purpose to live intentionally!

Intention begins with a Decision

EVERYDAY THAT WE awaken, we are faced with unlimited possibilities. Daily, there are choices before us that need to be made. Even if we choose not to make a choice, a decision not to choose has been made. What is a decision? Multiple online databases were consulted to develop a concise definition, one that is clear and understandable. A decision is a conclusion or resolution that is reached after weighing the positives versus negatives, benefits versus risks, and pain versus pleasure. We make so many decisions daily, in fact, we make a decision to make a decision. What is most disturbing is that often times, we make that decision, mindlessly, without even counting the costs, or considering the harvest or drought that may manifest in our lives. So, why are the decisions we make so important? Because, they have the power to change the course of your life. I recently had the pleasure of attending a conference with Dr. Cindy Trimm, and she gave an in-depth discussion on the power of decision. More specifically, she noted, each day we awaken with limitless possibilities, and every moment is pregnant with potential. Meaning that we were created as a "choosing" being, but where we most often fail, is that we are lost as to what decision to make, and instead of seeking God for the strategy, we choose not to decide-delaying the plan of God for our lives.[74]

As we embark upon each day, decisions meet us. Each time we make a choice, each time we make a decision, we are "cutting away" all other options that were present upon inception. Based on the decisions made, what we have accepted and what we have rejected, life manifests. So, what manifests in your life now, is a product of past and present decisions that you have made. The right to decide is a gift that even God, Himself, will not, and has not, taken away from humanity. Why? Because, as intelligent beings, we were born with the innate capacity to choose. However, what God, in His infinite wisdom has done, is availed Himself to be our spiritual guide, so that we have the ability to make prosperous and conducive decisions that bring life instead of destructive decisions that bring death. God leads and guides us daily, so that we will arrive at the destination that was pre-ordained for us.

There is so much power encompassed in the decisions that we make daily. Have you given any thought to the decisions that lie before you today? Have you surrendered your day to God and submitted to His will? Have you made a decision to become submitted to God today, knowing that He is the only PERFECT guide and in His Omniscience and Omnipresence, He can never lead you astray?

Remember, Proverbs 14:12 tells us that there is a way WHICH SEEMS right to a person, but its end is the way to death. Because of humanity's finite wisdom, we cannot rely on what seems right in our own eyes, but must seek God for His consultation. 1 Corinthians 1:25 (ESV)[75] states, "for the foolishness of God is wiser than human wisdom, and the weakness of God is stronger than human strength."[76] Therefore, we must rely on God, holistically, for ALL of our needs, wants, desires, dreams, OUR DECISIONS! Proverbs 3:5-6 states, "TRUST in the Lord with all of your heart, and do not rely on your own understanding. Acknowledge Him in all your ways, and He will make your paths straight." Remember, a person plans his course, but the Lord directs his steps. (Prov. 16:9, ESV)[77]

Are you committed to decision and intention today? Are you committed to speaking things into your life, after you have counted the cost, with an intention to remain faithful to the intention you have set? Are you ready for order, the power of faith, and the manifestation of the supernatural and extraordinary? Below are four tips for developing more intention into your day,

1. Seek God and pray for God's vision and will for your life. Once you abandon your will, and surrender all to God, God will show you His vision for your life.
2. Write the vision and make it plain. Those dreams and visions will resonate with your being once they are revealed. Write them down, pray over their manifestation, and allow your mind to feast on the roadmap that God gives you to achieve the vision.
3. Set daily intentions that work toward the vision. Remember, intentions are pacts between you and God. You MUST make them a priority. Intentions don't have to be big, they can be as simple as exercising, eating healthy, or getting rest. We must not compartmentalize God, but allow God's presence to permeate every sector of our

being and life.

4. Exercise commitment and unyielding dedication. When you plan your calendar, your intentions must be a priority. When you go throughout your day, your intentions must be a priority. Stop living by happenstance, and allow the intentionality of the Holy Spirit to manifest in your life.

Closing Motivation

The intentions of the heart belong to a man.
But, the answer of the tongue comes from the Lord.
All of the ways of a person seems right in his own opinion,
but the Lord weighs the motives.
Commit your works to the Lord,
And your plans will be established.

Proverbs 16:1-4 (NET)[78]

All you need is to surrender and submit to God! Then, every decision you make will be committed to God and your plans will be established.

Chapter 7:
FROM BITTER TO BEAUTIFUL

We delight in the beauty of the butterfly, but rarely admit the changes it has gone through to achieve that beauty —Dr. Maya Angelou

The Beautiful Unknown: A Reflection

*A*s I sit here just a few minutes shy of midnight, listening to the melodic Harold Judd, and watching the aerial views on my Apple TV, I find myself nostalgizing about my future. For a moment, I am displaced, dissociated with the present, walking in time to a place that only my spiritual sight allows me to experience. My mind is being stimulated by the beautiful unknown. I so long to be in a different place, a different time, a place unknown, but, yet, so *familiar, I feel as if I am standing there. The skyline is so serene. Is this what it is like to dream? To crave a reality and a destiny that God has planned, but you have not quite seen? I'm longing an unquenchable thirst to get where I have not, yet, been. I'm longing to tread the path to being lost in the wonder of inquisition and breathing the air of suspicion, being uncomfortable, but, yet, so free. Being inspired by God, and the vastness of His great mystery.*

I am here, flying on the back of an eagle; eyes wide open, as I hover over all that awaits me. I'm so excited that I want to jump, scared, but daring at the same time. So many times, God gives us the vision and the tools and instead of trusting and running with them, allowing to make manifest that which God desires for us to possess, we hold on to them and store them in a place of protection; and soon enough, we forget about them. The dream, the vision, is a tool. It's a telescope to which you have been granted permission to look through. You realize that what once seemed invisible is now visible. What once was impossible is now possible. Faith in action, right before your very eyes, and even if you only catch a small glimpse of the journey ahead, you realize that it has always been there. You had to change the lens you look through to see the beautiful unknown, is known, through revelation. Why swallow the seed that God gave you to plant; the seed that will create a harvest for you, and yet, because of your temporary situation and the hunger you feel, you swallow the dream? It is gone; never to return, and you are left just as hopeless as you began.

We must not cease to dream, because despite what you may believe, life is much more than what it seems. The only limitations placed on you are the limitations you place on yourself. If you are wondering why you have not yet achieved what it is you've dreamed, ask yourself. The answer to the question lies within you. God has done His part by revealing it to you. Stop blaming others, stop projecting, stop making excuses. Either do it, or don't! The holder of the key is you! You only hold the key as it is, because of God's trust. God gave the key to you. So, why are you afraid to take the journey into the beautiful unknown? Do you trust God enough that the vision that seems like a scene on a TV screen may one day be you, if you only believe? Is it too far-fetched to embrace the blessings of God, embrace the grace, the mercy, the pleasure, and the awe? What would it take for you to just take a step to commit to the journey, no matter the test? To set a goal date with Jesus, himself, to walk into the beautiful unknown.

The Journey from Bitter to Beautiful

THERE ARE SO many people in today's society that live a bitter life. Bitterness has become so prevalent that it has morphed into words associated with normalcy and is used to describe experiences that are life changing. We have phrases, such as, "bittersweet," "bitter end," and "a bitter pill to swallow." Bitterness does not have to be your state, in fact, it is possible to transcend from bitter to beautiful.

So what is bitterness, one might ask? According to the dictionary, bitter, in reference to taste, is considered to be sour, or pungent[79]. The same words can be used to describe someone of a bitter state, emotionally. They are said to be angry, unhappy, pessimistic, resentful, and unforgiving. This state of bitterness is usually triggered by an event or trauma that led to some emotional and spiritual damage. This transference of emotion from the pain or trauma onto everyday life and its subsequent interactions, manifest into what one would call, the bitter spirit. This leaves one discontented, which skews our perception and blocks our ability to see the purpose behind the pain, and the beauty just beyond the bitter. We encapsulate our entire lives to one moment, instead of remaining in the present and clinging tightly to the hope and optimism of a new day. Even though, in the present, we may see much pain and brokenness, we must hold fast to the consummation of all, so that we can, yet, taste the beauty that lies beyond. It is this beauty that many of our ancestors of old craved more than water on a desert-like day. For God is the satiation that promises to provide our soul, with the motivation necessary to press toward the prize, despite the bitter moments of life.

God has a way of opening our eyes to the wisdom in the lessons attached to the bitter moments in life. You will survive.

Life, and the many circumstances that meet you there, lead to a variety of feelings and emotions. While we expect everyday to be a day full of joy and happiness, the reality is, this is not true for everyday. Each day is new. We become complacent in our routines, treating every day as if it is the same, but it is not. This means that there are certain preparations that we must ensure in order for us to be able to embrace the beautiful moments, and endure the bitter ones. As followers of Christ, there is the expectation that we will live a life with no bumps, hurdles, or thorns. We expect perfection and accommodation from everything around us. This haughty expectation is the reason that Christians often renounce the faith when trials arise, because somewhere along the way their exposure was limited to only the prosperity gospel, and they were ill prepared for the cross-moments, the crucifixion moments, the moments where faith is the only sustaining power that helps you to maintain hope, because all else has failed.

Tell me, how did it come to pass that we expect only the good and beautiful, and we get so discouraged and dejected when our expectations are not met? Are we truly being honest when we say we trust God, and quote scriptures such as, "all things will work together for good to them that love the Lord and are called according to His purpose?" How is it that we can be super-spiritual when all is going well, but so easily forsake our belief and become indignant when a moment of oppression begins? Is it not God that makes all things beautiful? Is it not God that sends the character shaping winds of change into our lives to chip and carve away at the edges that needs to be refined? Is it not God' winds of change that blow some things out of our lives for a time, and utterly destroy other things in our lives that serve us no other purpose than to destroy or subvert the plan of God for our lives. Who told you the definition of beauty? What human led you to believe that they are the author of beauty and the standard to which it is judged? I contend with you today that beauty, and the definition of beauty, cannot be conjured by the mere mind of man, except only through the divine unction and supernatural sight revealed of the Holy Spirit.

Consider it pure joy, my brothers and sisters, whenever you face trials of many kinds, because you know that the testing of your faith produces perseverance. Let perseverance finish its work

> *so that you may be mature and complete, not lacking anything. (James 1: 1-2, NIV)*[80]

Most of what we define today as beautiful is attached to the enemy's devices of lust, fornication, and idolatry. Our perceived frailties and differences are seen as defects more than aspects of our uniqueness. We work so hard to mask ourselves because of the perception of others regarding our "flaws," not realizing they are not flaws at all. God's perception of beauty was conceptualized and made manifest through humanity. All of humanity is made in the image of God, and His response to you is that you are fearfully and wonderfully made, and that you are the apple of His eye.

God makes all things beautiful in His time.
Even the bitter things are made sweet.

Preparing to Shift

Inner Conflict

INNER CONFLICT IS like swinging from a pendulum. As we know, pendulums swing in two directions. They swing as far to the left, and as far to the right as they can, without making a full circle. How can you swing in two directions and ever expect to reach a destination? What is the purpose of a pendulum anyway, except to vacillate between two extremes, constantly? How can you resolve what you are not willing to face? How can you resolve the idiosyncrasies of you, when your extremes are imbued at the foundation of you? Many followers are like this today. We are, either, too righteous "in our own mind" that we are perfectionistic pretenders occupied with condemning others, or we feel so condemned subsisting from extreme to extreme. We are resistant to change because we know that change has a prerequisite of communing with God. Transformation requires exposure. Transformation requires forgiveness. Transformation is a byproduct of communing with God. So, we run from communion and never achieve transformation, only short lived resolutions and changes that disappear as quickly as they appeared. We run from authenticity. We fear communion, and we fear forgiveness of self. We become a tree with shallow roots and brittle branches, and the fruit of this fear leads to the adoption of a core belief that adduces that there is no room for God's righteousness to work or reside in U.S. This leads to the development of a habitual mind-set of condemnation; which is emotionally unhealthy, spirituality.

Oscillation. Erratic. The concomitant effects of what the scripture writers term as, "double minded," permeates the life of the one who is detached from the Almighty powersource. We become affixed between two extremes; stagnant with an internal scream that is as silent as night with no wind. Inertia leads to hopelessness and depression, and the stasis of death. Movement is essential. You must grapple to provide an answer to yourself about yourself, because no matter what you try, you can never escape yourself. In order to do this, you must seek God. You must become courageous and contend with the ruminating conflicts that plague your very existence. If you do not, the scriptures are clear that you will remain unstable in all of your ways and should not expect to receive anything from the Lord. Why is the struggle so difficult, especially when we have the very word of God speaking contrary to the inner thoughts yelling on the inside of us? Ask yourself: what was truth? Was my truth, truth? Or is the word of God truth? Yes, the word of God is, and yet, remains truth! What is the impetus for this dilemma that keeps us feuding within? The answer is simply this … .Sin.

So, for a moment, we are going to take a mental excursion, exploring humanity's struggle with sin. Most of us fail to understand the basic precept that we are born into a sinful nature, which is the Christian doctrine of the Fall of Man; and that we require salvation through Christ, alone, for remission of our many sins. Truth is clear that we all have sinned and fallen short of the Glory of God, and we must understand this, or else, become failures in our duty to be compassionate, but bold, soldiers for the cause of Christ. We have forgotten how to exercise self-compassion, which is part of the barrier to expressing compassion to others. This is the reason that we are turning from the Christian faith, due to our hypocritical and condemning attitude towards those inside and outside the faith; casting a negative light on the work that God has for all to do. The only remedy for the duality that wars within us, is Christ. Without Christ, there is no journey, there is no destination, there is no answer to the question that stops the pendulum from swinging.

The goal here today is two-fold; awareness, and preparation for the shift. Shifting is a complete transformation. It is holistic conversion of the mind; will, emotions, and body … a natural man overcome by the supernaturalness of God. Shifting requires two requisites: a full understanding of the unknown side or new, and a self-examination of our current state of mind and behavior. Consultation with God is a prerequisite for both aforementioned requisites. Let's examine the biblical example of Paul and his internal conflict to shed more light on humanity's struggle with duality.

In Romans chapter 7, verses 14-25; Paul provides us with an in-depth description of the Christians' struggle with sin. Paul deals with two mindsets here; one of condemnation, and one of haughtiness and self-pride. Paul, a Christian soldier, exemplifies the reality that even the chosen and elect, struggle daily with the battles against principalities, powers, and rules. We struggle daily with the sinful nature we are enslaved to. We struggle daily with self; the battle never seems to be won. This is why we run to opposite extremes, as the pendulum swings.

Pauls' Dilemma: A Monologue

PAUL REMINDS EACH of us that we were sold into sin-inheriting a sinful nature from the parents of our origination upon our inception into this life. And, though we know, in Christ, we are free from the penalty of sin and its power, we are still, yet, flesh; and we are NOT free from the presence or temptation of sin, and its varying possibilities.

As we examine self, and our very nature and behaviors,
We see that the sin-self still resides within.
I do not understand my own actions ...
I do not want. I want. I should not do, but I do ...
This is the daily plight of Christian soldiers, like me, and like you.

And, this nature,
It fights.
It wars.
It purposes to come without;
Causing mass confusion between the mind, the body, the actions,
attempting to dictate the choices you desire to choose.

But, I know what is right?
I think?
Do I know?
What am I comparing my behaviors to? Is it the Holy law of God?
Or the self-righteous law of man?
I'm not sure.
I'm so confused.

This is not me, this is not my desire.
I want to do what's right, but when I go to do it, I find myself doing–
the very thing that I've learned to spite.
This is not me. It's not me, but the sin nature,
So deeply rooted in me that won't free me.
Now, I'm condemned.
I can't get this thing right. I'm tired.
Should I still fight? Is this my eternal plight?

For nothing good dwells in my flesh.
I can, WILL what is right and still not do it.
Because, the good I want to do, no matter how hard I try,
I still can't seem to do it.

But, I always find myself doing that evil thing that I know I should not do.
It is not my innermost desire to commit these sins, but it is this sinful nature that I am enslaved to.

For, I delight in the law of God in my innermost self,
but I can feel, and I experience this.
The very things that I don't want to do, I do them; and the things I should do, I do NOT do them.

I can feel, and see vividly, this waring in my mind.
A vivid picture of a woman that I've so desired to leave behind, making me feel captive to the law of sin that dwells in me. I want out of this sinful waring that is fracturing the thoughts and impulses of my mind.
But, I can't seem to get out. In me, oh what a wretched wo-man I find.
Who will rescue me from this body of death, I cry.
I'm confused, I'm lost, I'm out of control, I'm blind.

But, then He opened my eyes; and with thanksgiving I hear my hearts cry.
Thanks be to God, through our Lord Jesus Christ.
He opened my mind.
And, I am reminded that I, with my flesh, I am slave to the law of

sin, but not with my spirit or my mind.
Because He lives within, I can and I will, this battle win.

This keeps me humbled and attuned at my current fleshly situation.
And helps me purpose to remain in holy introspection,
Knowing that there is no condemnation,
For those who are in Jesus Christ,
For the law of the spirit of life in Christ Jesus has set me free
From the law of sin, death, and its penalty.

Knowing this now, I can prepare for a mental and physical shift
Because Jesus is my Salvation!

Many want to deny the power of sin, but the reality is, sin is powerful. Sin is so powerful that, we, as Christians, wrestle with a divided self. We know the will of God. We set out on a path to be obedient and to do good, but we struggle to succeed. Conflict between the flesh and the spirit characterizes the Christian life; however, we can be assured of victory over sin. Through the process of sanctification, the blood of Jesus has restored, and can transform you; if you are ready for the transformation. You must be prepared to shift! The ongoing battle with sin is the earnest challenge in the life of the believer; however, you have a choice. You can stay in the fight, waring with this mindset of sin, or, you can declare the victory. How? First, by understanding there is no condemnation for those who are in Christ Jesus.

There is No Condemnation

CONDEMNATION, ACCORDING TO the Holman Illustrated Bible Dictionary[81], is an act of pronouncing someone guilty after weighing the evidence; making personal and critical judgments wrought with negative criticism. The only one qualified to issue any type of judgment, is Jesus. We all have sinned and fallen short of the Glory of God and since we were not selected to stand as judge nor jury, we should be careful not to possess a spirit of condemnation. 1 John 1:9 (NIV)[82] propounds that if we confess our sins, He is faithful and just to forgive our sins and to cleanse us from all wickedness. Philippians 1:6 (NIV)[83] reminds us that He who began a good work in you will complete it until the day of Jesus Christ.

Because we war with sin, we don't have to walk around with our head held down with an attitude of defeat. Through your living testimony, you can let another believer know that these sinful impulses will come, but through Christ the victory is assured. In Matthew 16:19, Jesus says, "I will give you the keys of the kingdom of heaven. Whatever you bind on earth will be bound in heaven and whatever you loose on earth will be loosed in heaven."[84]

Bind the enemy, bind the attack, and bind the denial that keeps you from acknowledging your sinful situation. Release God's word, release God's power, release the supernatural weaponry that is essential for spiritual warfare in this season. Shift from who you used to be, to who God has ordained you to be.

Do you know that, If God can use a man like Saul, it is not too late for you? Saul was:

-A liar.

-A deceiver.

-A Murderer.

-A Slanderer.

-Jealous and envious

Saul was cloaking and joking with the elite, with a strong desire to eradicate the Christians and the following Jews. But, look at the shift that occurred on the Damascus road; for, this is the place that Paul, the transformed man, was born. You must desire to shift from the old you (flesh) and purpose to PUT ON Christ.

Strategies for Transformation

Strategy #1: Embrace the Truth

SINCE WE KNOW there are none righteous, except Jesus, and there are none qualified to judge, except Jesus, you must purpose to stop allowing these self righteous and pharisaic "Christians," and the world condemn you. Take all that you are to the Lord in prayer and ask Him for forgiveness, and that thing you thought you couldn't get rid of, besetting sin, God will expose, purge, and grant you renewed strength to resist. Just a side note ... a condemned Christian is an oxymoron and is not a threat to Satan. Why? A condemned Christian is trapped in the confines of his/her own mind and poses no threat to the enemy. The enemy doesn't need to work to tempt you, you are so burdened down by your past sin, and so trapped by current sins, that you are static and feel that you are useless for the cause of Christ. A condemned person will not perform any function due to paralysis triggered by burdensome negativity and self-doubt. An altered reality is formed, and scales of blindness cover the eyes of their self-perception. Worthlessness becomes reality, because they cease to function. This is the desire of the enemy for you! There are so many who suffer from the plague of condemnation, they no longer need a real catastrophe to feel fear or sadness, because they create their own alternate reality in their mind. Unwilling to escape, they remain in this trap of planning for the 'what if,' years passing, and yet, they stand still, searching for the mirage, until one day, that which they desired, comes to pass. Remember to embrace the truth. Every word that proceeds from the mouth of God concening you is truth, the whole truth and nothing but TRUTH.

Strategy #2: Mind-Set

MAKE IT A daily practice to transform yourself by renewing your mind.

You may have heard this before, but I will say it again; the real battle is in the mind. Proverbs 23:7says, "For as he thinks in his heart; so is he."[85] Prayer is essential for transformation; you must talk to the Lord. He knows your every struggle. Stop going to everybody with your problems and take it to the Lord in prayer. Cease taking your burdens to the ones who cannot do anything but talk about you, and take it to the Lord in prayer because He will walk beside you. Renew your mind by reading and studying the word for yourself, develop your own relationship with the Lord, because blessed is the one who delights in the law of the Lord and who meditates on His law day and night. Setting your mind on things above, will free you from the cares of this world. It will free you from the worries of yesterday. It must be understood that knowledge of the law is not the answer, self-determination is not the answer, and becoming a Christian does not stamp out sin and temptation from a person's life. However, communion with God does remove our desire for sin. The more you commune with God, the more His will and desires becomes your will and desire. This is what mindset is all about. What the Lord desires for each of us to know today, is that, though, we were born into sin, and, though, we war with it daily, He has given us the power to overcome.

Paul is clear when he penned the letter to the Romans. In chapter 12 verse two (NKJV) Paul admonishes us "do not be conformed to this world; but be transformed by the renewing of your mind, that you may prove what is good and acceptable, and perfect will of God."[86] Transformation is the key to living a life aligned with God. Transformation is necessary for acquiring the endurance that is required to press toward the mark and attain the prize in Christ Jesus. While you may change, only God can transform. Seek to be transformed into the image of God and the authentic you He created.

Strategy #3: Armored DAILY:

IT IS IMPERATIVE that you suit up before you go into this world. Why?

We wrestle not against flesh and blood, but against principalities, against powers, against the rulers of the darkness of this age, against spiritual hosts of wickedness in heavenly places (Ephesians 6:12. NKJV)[87]. The goal of the enemy is to keep you from reaching the pre-ordained destination of your journey. We must be aware that nothing in life happens by happenstance, and the tactic of confusion, conflict, and condemnation are all tools to thwart your journey.

The enemy is looking for a way to penetrate your armor, and what better way than to cause confusion, self pity, and a spirit of condemnation? Suiting up in the full armor of God provides full provision for the journey. Protect and hide yourself under the shelter of His almighty wing by ensuring that you ask God to gird up your loins so that you will be able to STAND against all of the tactics of the enemy, and not fall for his devices.

Daily, we have to be prepared to shift by harkening to the voice and direction of God. We must purpose, daily, to shift our mental perceptions, shift our behavioral responses, shift our opinions, shift our actions and responses, and shift our words. We have to shift and control our tongues, and we have to shift our routine for the cause of Christ.

Are you prepared to shift today?

Salvation, justification, remediation, and sanctification comes from Christ, alone. Before you can experience this, you must prepare to shift. Yes, we know we were born into sin, and we know that sin nature lives on the inside of us, however, we also know, and are reminded that there is no condemnation for those who are in Christ Jesus. (Romans 1:8, NKJV) No condemnation does not mean believers are free from the struggle against sin, but that they are free from the SENTENCE of death and judgment on the last day.

I'm shifting. I'm transforming. I'm waiting on God.

Will everything be perfect after the shift? No! However, God will equip you with divine spiritual strategies for each circumstance you encounter; even if it is just to stand STILL.

Be Still and Know

MY SOUL, HAVE you pondered these words? "Be still and know." In the hour of distress, it seems you cannot hear the answers to your prayers. How often has the answer seemed to come much later? The heart heard no reply during the moment of its crying, its thunder, its earthquake, and its fire. But, once the crying stopped, once the stillness came, once your hand refrained from knocking on the iron gate, and once concern for the lives of others broke through the tragedy of your own life, the long awaited reply appeared. "You must rest, O soul, to receive your heart's desire. Slow the beating of your heart over concerns for your personal care. Place the storm of your individual troubles on God's altar of everyday trials, and the same night, the Lord will appear to you. His rainbow will extend across the subsiding flood, and in your stillness you will hear the everlasting music." -George Mattheson[88]

You must believe that it is settled, because God says so!

Nothing has ever been lost by keeping still! Understanding that often times our desire to "handle the situation" leads to hasty decisions we will later regret. Agitated responses have led to broken relationships, failed friendships, tense coworker interactions, and internal conflict. However, if you would only step back for a moment, delay your response for a time, put down the ego and the need to transform into the self defender, you will experience how different things appear through an unagitated eye. It is the Lord who will prevent the weapon from prospering and condemn the tongue that rises against you.

Be still, O My Soul

A transformative response:

WHAT WOULD HAPPEN, if hurtful actions or spoken words by a spouse were not met with a reply today?

What would happen, if that boss who continues to mistreat you and spread gossip about you, was met with avoidance today?

What would happen, if that friend who failed to keep the promise they made, was met with silent forgiveness today?

Just ask yourself, what would happen if you exercised control of your tongue and decided to allow no wrong word, slips of sarcasm, or uninhibited thoughts to part your lips and say…

Things that you will later wish had remained unsaid?

What would happen if you challenged and restructured the negative explanations posited in your head?

What would happen if you stopped and spoke peace to yourself, and decisively determined that not entering the conflict was much better for your health?

Every battle does not deserve an appearance. Allow the enemy to meet their shadow, alone.

In God's stillness, smile, and know vindication comes from God. The fight is fixed so the battle is already won.

If you keep your hands clean, and speak through the mouth of the redeemed,

you will learn that being still, with no wrong action, is all that you really need.

So, I invite you today, to practice silence. Practice not responding to hurt, pain, or disgust.

Practice joy, in the midst of trouble, knowing that it's your choice to entertain or avoid.

Practice writing your responses on a letter or a pad, and then sticking the note in a place where you can later review when you are not mad.

When you do this, you will find there is no need to send the note, and you may even question the feelings that triggered the hateful words that you wrote.

If it is an email, type it, but before you send it, save it as a draft.

So, you can return later and re-read it, reflect on it, and ensure that it appropriately articulates what you desire to say.

Again, when the anger has subsided and your soul is calm, you will find that you will not need it after all.

Silence. Stillness is the most powerful response conceivable at times.

Things look so differently in past-tense because we, then, recognize, understand, make allowances for, much more than you did before.

And, that which initially agitated you, fails to exert the power to steal your joy.

The choice to be still has the power to change your world.

―――――――――

Because, stillness and silence are great peacemakers.

―――――――――

Chapter 8:
LIVING TRUTH

I Shall Not Wander in the Dark

There are many times that we wander aimlessly into the day, with minds that are as dark as night; with no illumination, not even from the lesser light. We have no idea of what awaits us, no conceptualization or understanding of time, no purpose, and no real intention. Our day starts as "a hot mess!" We wake up late, have no idea what is on our calendar for the day, work off of the agenda of others, and at the close of the day, we question whether what we have accomplished was truly in line with our desires and aspirations. Where is the direction? Where is the focus? Where is the purpose? Where is the light of illumination from God?

Have you ever taken a moment to think about this recurring pattern and theme that surrounds your life? What are your behaviors saying about you? Have you ever engaged in a level of introspection so deep and authentic, that you realize that who you have become, is not who you envisioned yourself to be? Take a moment to recognize that navigating through life is like driving a ship. If you don't allow God to become the captain of your ship, if you don't plan your course with God's divine navigation, you will either arrive at a destination defined by someone else, or you will drift aimlessly nowhere! Either way, it is a destination truly unknown.

Have you ever asked yourself, "who am I?" and "what is my purpose?" Are you ready for a veracious answer? Maybe you just might find that you don't begin to measure up to the replica that God placed deep on the inside of you. Why? You have been chasing your will instead of His will. Check your pulse! Refocus to the rate and depth of your breath! Where is the love and self appreciation that you owe yourself? Where is the Y.O.U. that is created in the image of God? Whatever stumbling block you identify as a barrier, can be moved, with purposed intent.

It's okay to make the choice to begin … again. You have permission to fill the empty well with God ordained affirmations of your truly authentic character, versus the perpetuation and speculation of a society who has no conception of what it truly means to be Y.O.U. Choose today to look and see yourself in the mirror. Embrace your flaws as an improvement plan that preps you in this season for the journey that lies ahead. Choose today to hold yourself to a standard of grace, and not perfection, and realize that you are in competition with no one, but are a confirmation of the One! You must understand that the expectations of others, that you allow yourself to be entrapped by, were not placed on you by force! Instead of setting boundaries, healthy and holistic, you allowed those brick walled expectations of others to be placed around your territory! Now, you question both your ability, and growth. Others question your integrity, and your word. If this is your reality, take a step back and re-evaluate your destination. While the road is not going to be easy, the pleasure and satisfaction of doing what you love, should be enough motivation to get you through the stale and tiresome moments. Remember … the only thing that can be better is Y.O.U.

Truth

WHAT IS TRUTH? Truth is such an important concept, yet, quite difficult to conceptualize and put into words. Truth beholds the very essence of all things, and yet there are many who do not value the liberating authenticity that manifests when truth is in the room. God is truth. God's words are truth. Reality is truth.

John 14:6 affirms that Christ is the way, truth, and the life. Truth is revealed from the essence of our inner character that is most like God, and therefore, will permeate our inner character to our outer disposition. The closer we get to God, the more we search for God, the closer we come to truth; in fact, we become truth. We know now, what we did not know before. We can now discern with absolution, the real existence and the foundation of this existence. Being made in the image of God means that there is truth within us, and until we defile self through choice sin, we maintain that element of truth because we are constantly conforming to the image of Christ. The truth of inner life, that is twin to virtuous character, emerges not slowly over time, but rapidly because one touch, one encounter, one profession is the key to instant transformation.

Instead of transformation, we settle for rapid regression from supernatural to normality. Our righteousness, and the holiness ascribed to us from our creator is slowly tainted from the toxicity of this world. Everyday choices and/or decisions leave us stained with a deeper shade of corruption than whence we first began. We must be cleansed. In order to maintain truth, we must practice truth. Do you practice truth (you ask)? How you ask? Jesus must be invited into every area of our lives, including the deepest and darkest areas. When we invite Jesus in, He exposes the areas that need to be cleaned and restored; and, even, volunteers to do the dirty work of excavation and rehabilitation. While eviscerating the defilement of old unconfessed sin, God grants us the opportunity to purge and repent daily, calling to us, so that we can, again, be ushered to the potter's wheel of transformation. This is what it means to become more Christ-like. The more our inward and moral spheres are re-shaped into truth, the more our intellectual spheres and behaviors exude truth. This is a true profession of our faith, when we begin to live outwardly-the lives Christ called us to live. We live our truth. We become truth. Then we can proclaim, we are truth!

God is Truth. We need God now because we are running out of time.

The Lie of Time: A Reflective Monologue

As I sit next to the ocean and watch the waves crash on the shore, I notice that they are immediately pulled back to sea. It reminds me of the futility of life. We are here; vibrant, bold, converging on the shores of life with so much power and authority, and then, we wane back into the abyss of life, mixed in amongst the confusion of all of the waves. Until something boldly presses us forward, again, toward the shores, where we find that we repeat the same cycle of vibrancy, boldness, and power!

Waves cresting and crashing on the shore.

Why is this life so temporary? Why is our presence, in the grand scheme of things, only for a moment. In the twinkling of an eye, we find that our shine is dwindled; our flame is extinguished by the cycle or normalcy that causes insanity. I choose to run free from all of the expectations that trigger rumination attached to the frustrations of life. Forcing myself to abide by the customs of mediocrity and yet like the wave that crashes along the sea, I'm meant to be vibrant, bold, converging with power and authority.

But Time…

I WANT TO reflect for a moment on the lie of time. The reason for this topic, is because we are all guilty of thinking that if we just effectively manage our time, then we will be able to accomplish all that we need to accomplish. I often place things on my calendar and prioritize it based on deliverables, versus basing priority on what is valuable and meaningful to me. Sure, my career and education are important, but as I review my calendar, I failed to find any calendar entries for those things most important to me writing, exercise, meditation, rest, playing with my kids, and date night with the love of my life. No reservations for the part of me that creates forever through everlasting memories. This is very telling of how I prioritize my life, or the lack thereof. This demonstrates that I have become prey to the lie of time; thinking that I can, I will, but not today. We will do it tomorrow … right? This has led to historical burnout or simply, feelings of resentment, because my life, for a while, has been all work and no play. As I have evaluated the narratives in my story, I'm forced to face the question … With all that God created for our enjoyment, with all the glory reflected, and all that is placed on earth for us to see, am I enjoying all that God created to appease my senses, and rejuvenate my soul while I press through the toils, toward the goal He has set for me? I am reminded of Adam and Eve in the Garden of Eden and can't help but believe that we, too, are living in our own Eden; a garden, an oasis called Earth, that was fashioned for you and for me. The only thing we are missing is the immortality. But, while we are yet mortal, imbued with every sense to hear, taste, smell, touch, and see, we should seek to experience the ecstasy that God intended for humanity. Jesus shed much blood for you to experience the abundance of this life. For the blood of Christ, grants us both dominion and access, the only thing we are missing, is reestablishing the stewardship of TIME.

Teach me to number my days, so that I may gain a heart of wisdom. (Psalm 90:12)[89]

LIFE, AND ITS varying plight, has a way of extinguishing the time that has been granted. We become bitter because we have not effectively stewarded our time. We talk about all that we want to do, and what we should have done, but didn't do. Why regret your decisions when you made the choice to focus on productivity instead of prosperity, social chameleonism versus natural freedom, restriction versus liberation, to stay home in normalcy versus dancing in the ocean and night, with the lesser light, as you breathe the air that God strategically prepared for your lungs? Beginning today, as you breathe in (inhale), and breath out (exhale), with every breath, call His name. YWHW. Though we are finite, time with God will allow is to feel the infinite, and operate in His time.

Keep pressing. Keep breathing.

KING HEZEKIAH, WHEN he received the command to get his house in order because his time of death was near, understood how precious time was. He, also, showed us that if we step out on faith, and make our petition known to God, God may grant us more time. When Hezekiah received the command, he turned his face toward the wall, and prayed to the Lord saying, "remember now, O Lord, I pray, how I walked before you in TRUTH and with a loyal heart and have done what was good in your sight."(II King 20: 1-6, NKJV)[90] Hezekiah asked God to remember his stewardship over the time that was given to him, and prayed a petition unto God to grant more *time.* It is easier to pray to God and ask for more of something when you have a track record and examples to support and demonstrate your effective stewardship. Hezekiah was able to recount his walking before God in truth. How many of us can say that we are walking before God with a loyal heart and in truth? Why wouldn't God trust you with more if you have proven yourself faithful in the past? For the scripture says that the one who has much will be given more, and the one who has little, even that will be taken away from him. Hezekiah had much, and God granted his petition by adding 15 years to his life. God's response to his servant's prayer was, "I have heard your prayer, I have seen your tears, surely I will heal you."(II King 20:5, NKJV)[91]

God will grant more time, when we show ourselves faithful over time already given.

WILKINSON, IN HIS book, "*You Were Born for This*[92]," garnered much attention as he discussed the concept called, the "Risk Key." The Risk Key is a purposeful action you take, in spite of discomfort or fear, to exercise your faith during a miracle delivery. Faced with an unbridgeable gap between what you can do and what God clearly wants done, you take the risk to act anyway, depending on God to come through. When God supernaturally bridges the gap, He enables you to deliver His miracle and demonstrate His glory. As I read this quote, I pondered the number of times I felt in a position of confusion with regards to action. The confusion didn't exist because I lacked directions, it existed because there was a duel between the flesh and the spirit. During this duel, valuable time was wasted. It is hard to step out on faith when you have fear, but we must learn to press on anyway, with the assurance that God will bridge the gap. It is in the moments that our faith runs out, or the seemingly impossible stands in our way that our deliverance is accredited solely to God. We must allow for more miracles to happen in our lives. We must also share with those that we have influence, the power of God's provision as He truly makes up the difference. Give God your talent and your time, and watch God bridge the gap.

But Who Do You Say That I AM: Living Truth

IN THE 8TH chapter of the Gospel of Mark, we see Jesus amongst the gentiles in Decapolis after he had gone throughout the area of Tyre and Sidon preaching, proclaiming and healing many. Jesus has attracted a large following and, thus, we continue to see Jesus performing many miracles that include, feeding the four thousand men, plus women and children Gentiles, which is a separate occurrence from the feeding of the five thousand Jews. We also see the leaders of the Pharisees began to test and question Jesus, asking for a sign from heaven.

After the encounter with the multitudes, Jesus and his inner circle retreated via boat to an area of seclusion and Jesus begins to get into intimate conversations with disciples, seeking to expose them to the truth. He petitioned them to use their wisdom to see, hear, and behold all that he had done, not only for them, but also, for the thousands of individuals whom He had just left. He presents this dilemma that shows us that we can only experience truth, when our heart is open to truth. He asks his disciples, why are you talking about bread? Do you still not see or understand? Are your hearts hardened? Do you have eyes but fail to see, and ears but fail to hear? And, don't you remember?

After all of the healing, ministering, teaching and preaching amongst thousands of people, Jesus wanted to share himself with his disciples, but he could not share with them this truth until he established a deeper bond with them. As we can tell from the earlier questions Jesus posed to the disciples, they still had no real understanding of who Jesus was. The disciples needed to have a deep, personal understanding and appreciation of who Jesus was before He could share with them the pathway ahead, and invite them to follow Him in a life of devotion and sacrifice.

Then Jesus poses this question in Matthew 16: 13-19[93]: Who do people say that I am? Then, some answered, repeating what they heard the people in the crowds calling him. "John the Baptist," "Elijah," and "a prophet." But, Jesus who had heard the crowds interpretation of who he was, was curious to know what His inner circle thought of him. So, He asked a question that delved much deeper into the heart and soul of those who he counted as a part of his inner circle. "Who do you say that I am?" None were identified as responding, with the exception of Peter, who answered with a name that was descriptive and was a divine revelation. "You are Christ." Peter received the truth, because his spirit and his heart were open and hungry for the truth.

While this text doesn't elaborate as to if any others received the same divine revelation as Peter, we do know two things. (1) The other disciples were quick to repeat the perceptions and thoughts of others, but reluctant to offer a personal opinion as to their perception of whom Christ was; and (2) Peter was blessed because he received this revelation, and by receiving the revelation, was able to open the eyes of the other disciples to the true deity of Christ. It is important for us to be in the position of reception so that the Spirit can impart upon us the knowledge and wisdom of almighty God.

So Peter gives the name, You are the Christ. There is something powerful in the NAME. A name is something that is given to a person, that is a verbal representation or definition of who the person is. A name is a word or a set of words by which a person, place, or thing is addressed or referred to. It may be given due to familial significance, spiritual revelation, future proclamation as to the desired destiny of children and so on. However, because this name is assigned to a person, it bears some significance in describing the person. Name reveals truth. There is something deeper within the calling of the name, as each time you call a person by name, you are affirming who they are. The question was asked ... Who do you say that I am?

God was in the business of renaming folk throughout the bible for specified reasons, and each name came with a definition. He renamed Abram (exalted father) to Abraham (father of the multitude), Sarai (quarrelsome) to Sarah (Princess), Jacob to Israel (He who prevails with God), Simon, son of Bar-Jonah, to Peter, and so on. These name changes revealed a deeper understanding and purpose for the individual. So, when you called the name of Peter, you understood that Peter was the rock; and on that rock, the Church was built. Names were synonymous with character. When names are called, Jesus wanted something about the person's character to be revealed, and the light and purpose of the individual to shine through.

It's sad, today, that people give no thought to what they name their children-naming them after alcoholic beverages, cars, or material things. There is no significance, as in the days of old, when naming children. God was careful in giving names to his people, Ishmael, Isaac, Jesus. Names were significant. When you call the name of your children today, what are you really saying to them and others? What destiny are you shaping for your children by the words of your mouth? Moving away from names just briefly, there is something more detrimental than a name; it's called a label. We live in a society that is wrought with labels and titles. We put labels on people, just as the people placed labels on Jesus. Many of these labels were placed on Jesus, because they did not know who Jesus was. Unfamiliarity with someone results in assignment of labels. If you don't know me, you may attempt to describe me by your perception of me; sometimes this perception is based on my actions and sometimes it has nothing to do with my actions, but your judgments. Note that perception may be limited and untrue, at best. Instead of seeking to get to know someone, we tend to ask others the same questions Jesus asked his circle about themselves and others. We deeply desire to know what everyone is saying about us. What is everyone saying about me? We have begun to wear the labels and titles that people have placed on us. Then we live up to their expectations in the land of lost.

Words have as much power as we allow them to have. The greater our insecurity, the more these labels and titles and words shape us. So, we must decide, right now, to let go of the labels, titles, and names people have assigned to us, and those we have assigned to others. Do you need to undergo a name change so that God can reveal the truth of who you are? We must know that we are who God says we are, and God has an entirely different way of naming you; a name that embodies the essence of a whole new you. Truth. If you learn to live for an audience of one, you will not only discover who you are, but what you are, and what you were created to become. When God renames you, He is redefining and equipping you for His service.

Now, just as Jesus did, inquire about others perceptions of you, as they may be of some benefit. However, do not rely on the perceptions of others to define who you are. Each person, like Jesus, has an inner circle in which they can ask for wise counsel or expect correction. When you get stuck on "who people say that you are," you may lose sight of who you are and who God created you to be. Jesus did not get stuck on the people's wavering and blinded perceptions of who He was. Despite all the good He had done, many still had a negative perception of who He was.

The same will be true for you.

Learning and understanding yourself begins with knowing and understanding who God is. Who you are is defined ONLY by God. It is not enough to know what other people have to say about Jesus, we must know God for ourselves, because He is the revealer of truth. This is what Hezekiah was talking about. Hezekiah's request was granted, because his heart was loyal to God. We get to know God by accepting him, committing to him, drawing closer to Him, and then, understanding him. When Peter answered the question, he responded with the name God, the Father, had given – Jesus Christ; Yeshua HaMashiach. And, with that name, came meaning … All powerful God and Son of the living God.

What is your name?
What does your name mean?
Is your name descriptive of who God designed for you to be?
What labels have you been given?
Are these labels definitive of who you are?

Beginning today we are taking a bold stand. As God asks us the question, "Who do you say that I am," we must be open to God's revelatory power. After God has revealed Himself to us, we can then ask, Lord, who do you say that I am? What would you have us to be? What is the name by which you desire for us to be called? Stop asking other people to define you; go to the source and ask Jesus. Ask Him, "who do you say that I am?" And, He will answer, letting you know exactly who you were created to be.

You are in a league of your own ... literally! With over 7.4 billion people in the world, there is not another you! So, take off the carefully constructed image called perfection, that has left you wandering on the dark road to someone else's destination. It's okay to live in the light! Its okay to be Y.O.U. No longer do you have to hide those aspects of you that you feel are not perfect in the sight of others. If it is permission that you need, I grant it to you now. Today, I give you permission to be authentically Y.O.U.

Authentically Y.O.U.

Authenticity relates to the ability to stand for, embrace, and pursue that which is meaningful, valuable, and an accurate representation of who or what an individual believes him or herself to be. Authenticity is truth. What do you stand for? What is meaningful and valuable to you? Are you representing Y.O.U or is that, yet, another mask we see?

In the face of a societal standard that is biased towards the diversity that is inherent among us, impeding the ability and agility of accepting without judgment, the varying differences and the humor God felt in creating humanity; hold up your banner of grace and light! Don't strive for the darkness of perfection, strive for the light of self-exploration, self-appreciation, and self-love! Feeling worthy to simply be you! Let self love permeate your being, allow self acceptance, and godly alignment to seep from your pores! Walk with the sway of the wind, head held high, shoulders broad, because you are propped by almighty God!

Today, God is introducing you to truth and giving you a new name, ridding you of the labels. We are replacing:

Ugly with beautiful.

Stupid with intelligent.

Not good enough to more than a conqueror through Christ who is our strength.

Mistake with purposed and predestined before the foundation of the world.

Forgotten with loved and highly favored.

Useless with diligent and productive.

Failure with unlimited success.

Evil with holy and righteous through the blood.

Deceptive with trustworthy.

Defiant and hard headed with obedient.

Careless with discerning and wise.

I declare and decree today, that God has given you a new name.

After Peter has confirmed who Jesus was, we see in the proceeding verses, Jesus begins to engage in sharing intimate secrets about his life and ministry, specifically the foretelling of His betrayal, death, and resurrection. He also expressed to them what they must do to become true followers of the truth. If we become intimate with Christ, He will share intimate details with us as well. This is what we must do to know and understand who Jesus is and who we are:

1. **Ask your creator.** Petition Him and He will answer.
2. **Deny self.** Deny all of the labels and expectations this world has placed on you.
3. **Take up your cross.** Walk in the newfound name and its descriptors as assigned by your creator. He knows you best.
4. **Follow Jesus.** To follow, means to walk behind while being guided; to look forward to; to lean to for guidance. God is leading you to the truth of who He is and the truth of who you are.

Following God is the ultimate submission to Truth; for He is Truth. Make an intentional choice! Affirm, I SHALL NOT wander in the dark! You are one purposed decision away from the one change that is necessary to change everything!

Ultimate Submission

WALK WITH ME now on a journey far away from home, in a world unknown.

And, while on that journey, though your only intent was to give, all you received was selfishness, deceit, blasphemy, disrespect. Everywhere you turn, you are met with ridicule, false accusations, unjust trials, beaten and abused.

Imagine being the Messiah, walking on earth with your creation; and only being able to communicate your true identity to a humble few.

And, while among them you ponder whether they even have an understanding of who you are, and the great sacrifice made for you to be with them walking side by side.

Imagine our Savior who came unto His own and His own received Him not.

And, yet, He decided to tarry, to provide an example of what should be and what should NOT.

After all of the pain, heartache, and frustration; after all of the expended compassion, and unconditional love;

After all the sins of the world were placed onto His shoulders: every sin, for every man, for all eternity;

He still went to the cross!

On this cross, feeling, for a moment, forsaken by His heavenly Father, His back turned while the blood stained iniquity covered His dear, innocent son. IMAGINE–AFTER ALL OF THIS–He was, then, able to commit His Spirit,

to return home to a place with his Father and friends. His rightful place.

A PLACE where He belonged.

A place of vindication, a place of ultimate protection, a place where the scorn of evil and rejection is no longer a possible subjection.

A place where everyone is smiling and joy truly unfolds. A final and eternal resting place in the hands of the One that He loves. A place … O what a place that we all one day hope to be. But, in order to arrive,
while on this side, we must Submit …

To God's will,
To doing it God's Way,
To walking the journey with Him each and every day.
To remaining fervent, to the call for which you have been called.
To give your all to Him. Surrendered. Because anything short of this, is to give nothing at all.

Jesus taught us, on this side, what it meant to truly yield; not to our desires, but only to do our master's will.
To slow down and to listen; and to humbly remain still.
Until
He gives you directions to work, speak, preach, and to heal.

Look to Jesus and see all that our Savior endured; it wasn't for His benefit, but because of His un-matchless love for you. There is no safer place, no more trusting place, no more fulfilling place to be than in the hands of our Heavenly Father. It is because of Jesus, and His ultimate show of unconditional love, we can now make this declaration … I choose Truth. I submit, God, to you.

Chapter 9:
ALIGNED AND SYNERGIZED

"Christ is the originator and the upholder of the universe. In Him, the power of God, the universe, became an actual, real thing, perceptible to others; and in Him, it consists, or holds together, from hour to hour. The steady will of Christ constitutes the law of the universe and makes it a cosmos instead of a chaos, just as His will brought it into being in the beginning." -A. H. Strong[94]

Align with God and Dream

True vision begins once we are in alignment with God, as He is the inspirer of all divine dreams. Before the foundation of the world, God had a plan with you in mind. Not only did that plan include a physical manifestation, your eyes, nose, ears, the bend of your hips and your hairline; it also consisted of your gifts, talents, your desires, your satiations, which all makeup your purpose. The purpose that God has for you is deeply embedded in the core of who you are, and in order for that dream to travel from the subconscious and spiritual aspect of self to the conscious and natural part of self, one must take the necessary and appropriate time to dream.

What does it mean to dream? If we think about dreaming in context, we can extrapolate a few lessons on how to transform dreaming from the night life to our active wake life. At night, when we are at our most calm and vulnerable state, the conscious mind is silenced in a state of rest and restoration. During this time, our subconscious mind is given free reign and liberty to express the deepest aspects of self. Each night, our mind is set free, like an animal in the wild, to not only process what has occurred during the day, but to dissect and explore every aspect of it. Our mind is sent on a journey to explore the truth within ourselves and to highlight the inconsistencies of both our inner and outer being. Sometimes, the subconscious pulls from multiple differing scenarios, meshing them all together into a conglomeration that creates a dream that, in the wake life, just wouldn't make sense. In reality, this dream entails some aspect of you in every scene, but we dismiss it as fictional or something watched on television. Isn't it interesting how free we are when the conscious mind is unable to control the very instinct of our humanity? I mean, think about it, we can be anyone we desire to be in our dreams. We can fly, write books, sing, dance, survive death experiences … all in our dreams. In the dream, we can operate in supernatural power, we experience tense episodes of love and affection, we have all that we really desire, and some of what we do not, in our dreams. Why, then, can we not live in a state of such freedom in our wake and conscious life? Why are we so restricted and resistant in what we can and cannot accomplish, where we can and can not go, and with whom we can and cannot share our being? The conscious life, is much less exciting than our dream life. But, there is something profound about the dream state. God communicates with us more clearly when we are dreaming. Why does God communicate with us through dreams more often than through visions? Note that there is a difference. One only possesses the ability to have a vision after they have mastered the ability to dream. Dreaming requires a cessation of the conscious mind and an activation of the subconscious spiritual mind. However, during a vision, one has the ability to dream consciously, but it is no longer called a dream; it is now a vision. When you can see the purpose and plan that God has for your life, when you can see warnings, promises, the future, and the past all while you are conscious, this signifies a higher level of alignment with God.

Life often brings into our path multiple stimuli. We must remember that the enemy is the author of deception, and one of his most artful tools is to keep you mentally distracted and BUSY. During this time of busyness, your mind is so occupied, there are no moments of rest and calm. There are minimal moments, at best, to engage in thought beyond the here and now. Our mind is fixed and focused on the tasks that lie ahead, and because preoccupation abounds, there is no time, and no desire to dream. Consciously, we have the ability to make decisions. We have the ability to entertain or ignore. We have the ability to defy instinct. We have the ability to quench the spirit and ignore the voice of God. God's voice is so gentle, it requires a mind that is intently focused in expectation of receptivity. You cannot be parsed. Dreaming requires the total being; not just one piece of you. Dreaming requires intentional focus which is hard for most of us to do.

Because of the level of control we exert in our conscious state, God often interjects His will and desire for your life when we are open to hearing and receiving. This often occurs when we are sleeping; when you are not consciously in control. When you have relinquished control during your nighttime rest, God is able to, then, communicate to His creation, gently, by allowing you to hear His voice and experience His desire from within. This supernatural ability to commune with God, was implanted within you at conception. It is from His guiding voice that the true you begins to manifest. The seed implanted by His command, dictates what makes you feel happiness and sadness, what you find pleasurable, whether you are a lawyer or a teacher, your favorite color, and how you interact with others. This seed of potential, if watered, will grow into your purpose that will be experienced, first, inwardly, and, then, outwardly. The battle that most people have, is that they experience the inward manifestation of the dream, but because of circumstances and life issues, roles, relationships, distractions, and expectations, we will not allow the purpose to manifest in its outward form. This outward manifestation of the dream is important. You will never feel fulfilled until you are aligned, inwardly and outwardly. You will never feel purpose, until this seed, deeply implanted on the inside of you, is allowed to take root, grow, and branch out. If you continue to consciously kill your dream, you will never grow to your fullest potential. God sees you as so much bigger than you are! However, somewhere along the way, someone or maybe even multiple people, imparted into us a different dream, a dream of mediocrity. They may have even implanted their dream because of expectations they have of you that are closely tied to their own internal selfishness. Wrapped up in their "dream" of you, are rewards to be reaped for their own benefit. We must abandon the dreams of others, and ensure that we are aligned with God and His dream. We must be very careful to whom we lend our ears, our eyes, and our time, because they are unknowingly implanting seeds into your life that, if you are not careful, will overgrow and smother the dream that God implanted even before conception.

Many of us do not know God's true purpose for our lives, because the enemy has made it his personal mission to choke the life from our seeds. This reminds me of the parable of the wheat and the tares. Both grow together, but in due time, God will do the separating. The original seed that is aligned with God's purpose is growing in the same garden of seeds implanted by your parents, your friends, your mate, strangers, colleagues, co-workers, and, yes, even your enemies. All of these seeds planted-some knowingly and some unknowingly-at different times during your life, are now all growing together in your heart and in your mind. So many different options, so many different choices, so many differing expectations and outcomes; how do we know which one is our ordained dream? This is another tactic that is the bait of Satan. Yes, all of the seeds and options look great. You may even stand to benefit some rewards from these seeds, but they will, in no way, compare to the plans of God. We take too many cheap alternatives to God's plan and purpose for our lives, because we abandon the ability to conceptualize. We miss out on the manifestation of the dream because we lose faith. Someone has tricked us into believing that we cannot achieve what others have achieved. We forsake the possibility that God really can do exceedingly and abundantly above all that we can ever ask or think. Who led you to believe that God was "small?" I say this because we become complacent with mediocrity, and have small self-expectations, and even smaller God-expectations. We deduce the power of God into our mere expectations, and then get upset with God when we look back over our lives with sadness and irritability that we never achieved our fullest potential, nor manifested the purpose that God predestined for us.

Don't blame God, place the accountability where it truly belongs.

What a waste, I think to myself, had Maya Angelou, Dr. Martin Luther King, and others not achieved their purpose. Many of us have freedoms and enjoy luxuries, such as free education and the right to fellowship as we so desire, because of the purpose manifested in the lives of others. What if they deduced God to mediocrity? What if they had disregarded the need to nurture the growth of the inner seed that God supplanted the moment we were mentally conceived in His being? What if they had not aligned themselves with God, allowed the dream to become a vision, and the vision a reality? What if, they had not asked God to harvest them so that all other seeds ,along with its growth, that was not of God, be plucked out? What if our obedience is directly attached to someone else? Others are impacted by your public and private decisions. When you chose to quench your purpose and destiny, something in the universe is either not achieved, or God will reassign your purpose to another whom He is fashioning. Aligning with God for the manifestation of your dream is essential. Life depends on it ... literally. This life is bigger than YOU. It supersedes YOU. Your destiny is not just for YOU. Souls are saved, eternal life is obtained, hearts are healed, hungry stomachs are fed, injustices are illuminated, freedom is won! You, yes YOU, were born for such a time as this. You were not created by happenstance. It took divine hands, to create the unique design called you. Now be Y.O.U! Align with God, dream, and birth forth what God has predestined and pre-ordained for you to do!

Facing the Preparational Opposition

The opposition serves only one purpose, to refine you and make you greater! Opposition does not possess the capacity to destroy you!

IT'S AMAZING THE anxiety that is provoked when we face situations and circumstances of opposition. There is this expectation that life should be trouble free, and this entitlement perspective that many have adopted, has lead to the belief that adversity is not normal, and that life should give one everything they want and more. Opposition, has reshaped lives, ended careers, destroyed relationships, and contributed to the pandemic of negative self concept and low self-esteem. The question is why? Does opposition really possess this much power? The power to tear down relationships and accomplishments that took decades to create and build? Does opposition really have the power to shift your atmosphere so much so, that it causes you to question the very foundation on which you now stand, and the foundation on which you were created? I posit today, that it is not opposition, but our understanding of opposition wherein lies the problem. What would happen if we changed our perception regarding opposition; viewing it from the perspective of a challenge and test that is preparational in intent, and will allow us to refine self and our core concepts, so that we as individuals grow beyond measure?

Reality is:

> Those closest to you are those who hurt you, and can provide the greatest degree of opposition.
> Remembering that it wasn't strangers that threw Joseph in the pit, it was his brothers.
> It was not the unbelievers that called for the crucifixion of Jesus, it was the leaders: Pharisees, Saducees, and the religious leaders of that day, and those who were guised as friends.

As soon as Jesus' assignment was revealed and the heavens rolled back, and the dove descended, and God announced, "This is my beloved Son in whom I am well pleased," His enemy was revealed. The opposition, or shall I say, the TEST began, and He was led into the desert to be tempted. When your assignment is revealed, so is your enemy. The opposition strengthens when you are walking in your calling and preparing for elevation. When you see the enemy, when you see opposition, that means this season is coming to a close and you are about to enter a new season. The enemy's presence is an indicator that God is planning movement.

Is there something to be gained from opposition? Yes, strength, courage, and the effective ability to problem solve and persevere. Does opposition possess the capacity to cancel your destiny? No, but your response to the opposition can possess a lasting impact, which can threaten your destiny, and alter the timing and intensity of your role when you arrive. We must view opposition from a perseverance and strengths based perspective, knowing that my ability to pass this test will provide me with preparational lessons that will benefit me for years to come.

The answer to opposition is not always easy. However, with the right mindset and a clear understanding of the purpose of opposition, we can tailor our responses for our benefit. Answering opposition requires five essential ingredients: prayer, self-analysis, obedience, perseverance, and self-control.

-In prayer, the opposition is revealed as God always seeks to prepare His children. The goal here is to be attentive and listen!

-When self-analyzing, one is able to discern the role opposition will play in not only their lives, but the lives of others around them.

-Self-analysis affords you with the opportunity of weighing your options to a variety of tactics from the enemy, so that you can work with God on a battle strategy, and tailor your response in advance. When, through discernment, you prepare and weigh the options before you, you can then seek to obey God's desired response for you in the season of opposition. Truly, many who respond negatively, do so out of lack of preparation, and lack of self-control. When you are prepared, your arsenal becomes more diverse, and your choices aligned with the exemplary power to honor God even in the midst of your circumstances.

-When you are obedient, you are able to persevere or outlast the enemy. Why? Because your reinforcement, your motivation, and your dedication is to almighty God. He will prepare you to outlast any opposition you may face. He will also give you the ability and agility to dodge many of the traps and snares set before you; because through your spiritual eye, you can see what is invisible to the naked eye.

-Self-control is listed last, but is certainly not the least. These five essentials began with prayer, but are propped and maintained by self-control. While you may not possess the power to control anyone else, GOD and YOU are the only ones who possess the power to dictate your behavioral responses, unless you relinquish that power and control to another. Remembering this … you must never freely give away the keys that open the door to your life, your thoughts, and your behaviors. These keys must be tightly grasped, and visible to only those with whom you trust. Keys include your passions, convictions, dreams, life goals, and triggers attached to your feelings. If you expose these, the enemy will use them to penetrate your environment, intrude your privacy, dismantle your comfort zone, and take over your life.

There are also times when the ability to ignore is essential. Assessment of the time dedicated to opposition is the key, as time is valuable and must not be wasted on senseless distractions. We are to be distracted by our future and not distracted by meaningless things that do not deserve attention.

Matt 10:16-17; 19 (NIV)[95] states, I am sending you out as a sheep among wolves. Therefore be shrewd as snakes and harmless as doves. But beware of men, for they will deliver you over to the courts and flog you in their synagogues. When they deliver you over, do not be anxious how you are to speak or what you are to say, for what you are to say will be given to you in that hour."

Opposition will come. False accusations, plots, plans, and pre-prepped graves will be the fate of men for you. We must then remember, they don't hate you, they hate the God in you. They hate that you have favor! They don't hate you, they hate what God is doing for you! It's not about you, it's about the God in you.

But, he who endures until the end, will be saved. Endure in prayer! Endure with self-control! Endure, PERSEVERE in obedience! Endure until the end of this test, and you will find yourself crossing the Jordan into your promised destination!

God is talking ...

Do You Know His Voice?

CAN THE LORD talk to you in confidence? Can He have an intimate conversation with you, and only you? Can He share His thoughts and plans, not only about you, but about the world, as well, and you never utter one word without His permission? Can the Lord engage you in a private conversation, and share all of His frustrations, His pain, His joys, His love, His angst? Or are you so two-faced, that you would betray God, by sharing what He commands to be kept secret, even to those who are closest to your heart?

Are you free to listen? Can God have one minute of your time? Can you pencil Him in on your calendar, or are you too busy? Is He not important enough to prioritize?

The Lord is not asking you to bear His burdens, but sometimes He likes to talk. He loves to share His heart, His will and His thoughts with us. He likes to walk and talk with you in the cool of the day, like He did Adam and Eve; but are you listening? What a privilege for God to talk to you, to trust you with His secrets. What a privilege it is to be selected and chosen as the witness while God's shares His burdens. Just as we, in humanity, feel the need to commune, talk, and share companionship, God desires to share this with His creation. Communion is why God created man. Communion is why God walked and talked with Adam and Eve in the garden, daily. Communion is why God sought Adam and Eve after they had sinned. God seeks to commune with you today. What are three things you can do today to commune with God, so that He can reveal to you the desires of His heart?

Intimacy: The voice of the Lord

Job 33:14: "For God speaks in one way, and in two, though man does not perceive it."[96]

WE KNOW THAT from the beginning of time, God has communed with and communicated with humanity. Made in the image of God, we were endowed with five senses, each able to understand the communicative devices, or the voice of God. Why do I say communicative devices? When you research voice, you will find that the goal of the voice is for the purpose of communicating. Audible voice is a sound produced by the larynx that makes a pitch or a tone. With this pitch or tone, words are relayed that provide expression of the mind, articulating some command, instruction, revelation, or utterance. There are however, times where the voice or expression of the mind is communicated in methods other than the audible voice. We know that God is always speaking, however are you able to recognize the voice of God?

In John Eckhardt's book entitled, *"The Prophets Manual,*[97]*"* he notes that every believer should EXPECT to, not only hear the voice of God, but to also speak as the oracle of God. In fact, Dallas Willard[98] notes that the material world, in which we are placed by God, permits God to be nearer to us, even more than our own eyes, ears, and brain are near. God does not have to go through physical intermediaries of any sort to reach us, though, on some occasions he obviously chooses to do so.

However, if you did a cursory poll of those whom you encountered on a daily basis, you would find that many will share that they have never heard God speak to them personally, and more unsettling, are the confessions that they would not know God's voice or method of communication if He did speak. Scripture tells us that it is God, and God alone, that should direct the path of every believer, therefore, it is imperative that we know His voice.

We say that we are Christian, but do not hear the voice of God. Is this possible?

John 10: 27-28 states, "My sheep hear my voice, and I know them, and they follow me. I give them eternal life, and they will never perish, and no one will snatch them out of my hand."[99]

How can you follow a God, whose method of communication, you cannot understand?

Perhaps, we do not hear the voice, because we do not expect to hear it. We so desire to be the master of our own lives and our own fate, and thus, the only voice we expect to hear, and the only voice we desire to hear, is that of our own or the praises of man. We see God's voice as an intrusion on our wills and desires, and we only desire God's opinion and intervention when things are going wrong, or we find ourselves in a dilemma that we cannot escape. But, God's personal creatures, whether angelic or human, are also guided by His intimate communication of his intentions and thoughts.

God does indeed guide us in many ways. His guidance can manifest in special acts of intervention in our lives, or by His general providential ordering of the world. In my opinion, His direct communication with us, by word and by shared activity, is the most important part. This is because we are to become the temple of God, one that actively understands and cooperates with God's purposes, one that is willing inhabited. Being a temple requires communion between ourselves and our God.

God is always guiding, as life would be quite strange if He didn't. The Psalmist asks, "He that planted the ear, shall he not hear? He that formed the eyes, shall he not see?" (Ps. 94:9, ESV)[100] And, I ask, "He that made the tongue and gave us power to communicate with one another, shall he not speak and communicate with us?" I do not believe that God our Father is a mute, non communicative impersonality.

Many would associate the audible voice and commands of God to auditory hallucinations or delusions that would send one into a state of panic or fear. However, communing with God is not mental illness, it is not hallucinating, and it is not substance exposed behavior. It is simply the creation communicating with the creator. Anyone who cannot understand this, has no relationship with God.

It is clear that one person's conscious concentration on another, frequently evokes a reciprocal awareness. Since this is known to be true among human beings, we should not be surprised that God's attention to us should result in our reciprocal awareness of God's presence.

Are we in a position to hear? The fact that we do not hear God does not mean that God is not speaking to us. It may mean that we are not attuned and aligned to the communicative strategies of God. We must, then, seek our God and seek to hear His voice, or else expect to remain lost ... forever.

It All Began in the Garden

HYMNOLOGIST C. AUSTIN Miles (1912), penned this hymn:

> *I come to the garden alone,*
> *While the dew is still on the roses, and the voice I hear, falling on my ear.*
> *The Son of God discloses.*
> *And He walks with me and He talks with me*
> *And He tells me that I am his own*
> *And the joy we share as we tarry there,*
> *None other has ever known.*
> *He speaks, and the sound of His voice is so sweet, the birds hush their singing*
> *And the melody that He gave to me, within my heart is ringing*
> *I'd stay in the garden with Him,*
> *Though the night around me be falling,*
> *but he bids me go, through the voice of woe,*
> *His voice to me is calling ... .*

Gardens are a place of growth, care, transition, and nurturing. Gardens are a place of cultivation, where you are under the watchful care of a farmer who is skilled in making you grow and reach maturity. Gardens are the place of origination, the place of cultivation, the place of nourishment. Our garden is in the presence of God. There is SOMETHING SPECIAL ABOUT A GARDEN. THE SEED OF LIFE IS PLANTED IN THE GARDEN.

The garden is synonymous with God, the origin and giver of life. Life began in the garden-when God Almighty planted the seed of His image into the very heart of humanity. God took his time and formed man from the dust of the ground, and blew into his nostrils the breath of life. God placed Adam in his presence, in the garden. God trusted humanity with his greatest gift; His heart, and the secrets within. God entrusted humanity with a piece of His will.

It was in the garden, that not only man's life began, but all life; and all that was necessary to sustain life. The scripture states that pleasant and sustaining trees and shrubs were placed in the garden, beautiful for the sight and good for the body. It was in the garden that Adam and Eve had intimate contact with God Almighty. God walked with them and talked with them. God shared with them His heart, and gave them a puzzle piece. Each one of you have, at the foundation of your heart, a piece of the puzzle that together forms the divine plan of God that was given to you at conception.

You carry in you a precious gift; the indwelling of Almighty God, and you are a bearer of His image. God desires to walk with you.

Anointing and Preparation happens in the Garden

THE GARDEN AT Gethsemane, a place whose name literally means, "oil press," is located on a slope of the Mount of Olives just across the Kidron Valley from Jerusalem. A garden of ancient olive trees stands there to this day.

When Jesus needed His father the most, when He needed to hear His voice, He went to the garden. It was in the garden that the Father gave His son what was needed to sustain life, and not just for His life, but ALL life. It was here in this garden, that the Father anointed His Son and gave Him all that was necessary to ensure the hardship and the humiliation that was about to come His way. He gave His son the power of endurance, a deafened ear, a forgiving heart, and an obedient spirit to walk the journey ahead of Him, all while remaining faithful to the Father's will, in spite of, what it looked like and felt like.

Jesus plead to His Father three times in this Garden, releasing all of His fears, worries, and anxieties, praying so fervently, that He began to sweat drops of blood. Why did Jesus go to the garden to pray? As stated earlier, the garden is where the originator of life Is! It is symbolically representative of the originator of all life. Jesus placed himself in the presence of His Heavenly Father. When His Father, the farmer, arrived and cultivated Him, prepared Him, pruned Him, and nourished Him for the mission, His humanity left Him and the Divine overtook Him; for no human could have endured all that Christ endured before He made it to the cross; except they be equipped by God.

God equipped Jesus with everything He needed to accomplish the mission, and to achieve His divine purpose and the Father's will. This divine aid ensured that He was able to see the mission to the end.

On this journey, you, too, will carry a cross. When you choose to carry your cross, the journey won't be easy. When human frailties fail you, it is in the garden that you draw strength. It is in the garden, where you must choose to place yourself in the presence of God, and allow God to give you the supernatural strength to do His will.

Not only can we pray for strength in the garden, we can expect new life to begin in the garden.

Resurrected Life-New Life begins in the Garden

John 19:41:

"Now in the place where He was crucified, there was a garden; and in the garden a new sepulcher, wherein was never man yet laid."[101]

JESUS WAS LAID in a borrowed tomb in a garden, and rose to new life in a garden. This is a reminder that life is not only sustained but new life begins in the garden. It is at the place of origin, that we can expect to lay down all the troubles and hardships of life, and expect to be nourished. It is in the garden that we can speak and expect that which we have spoken to manifest. There is power in the garden to grow all good things, by simply planting a seed, God waters and gives the increase.

Garden, a place of cultivation and nourishment when you are in a helpless state.

It is in the garden that God will walk with you, like He did Adam and Eve in the cool of the day.

It is in the garden that God will talk with you.

It is in the Garden that God will comfort you and give you the strength to press on toward the mark of the high calling in Christ Jesus.

It is in the Garden that God will remind you that you are His own, and it is He that is the Farmer, it is He that is the master potter.

It is in the Garden that God will give you **NEW LIFE** and **ETERNAL LIFE**.

It is in the garden that you can align and become synergized with the Great I AM. It is in the "Us-ness that we experience an exhaustive crazy love for our God."

Chapter 10:
UNCONDITIONAL LOVE

Exhaustive-Crazy Love for God: A Monologue

One night as I slept, I found myself in a full-fledged battle with the one person closest to me. The dream was so vivid and physically taxing, that I woke up the next morning, body feeling as if I had just went to the battle of a lifetime.

Though I told myself it was a dream, mentally and physically, that was not the case. This was more than a dream. It was a battle with the enemy, wearing the face of the one I loved, reminding me that if we are not holistically protected, the enemy will work to penetrate even those closest to our hearts. Why this dream? Why this night? Why this particular loved one? The message was very clear; the enemy wanted a battle, and that is simply what he received. God, in His faithfulness and protection, allows us to see beyond what appears to be real. He allows us to visually penetrate that which is in *front of us through His keen analytical eyes, and to decipher the moral code and the heart of those around us. Even in a dream, we are equipped with the 20/20 vision and insight to be able to separate masking from authenticity, real from fake, counterfeit from genuine, phony from purity. Why does God allow us to see that which is before us? Why is it so important for God to allow us to see through His eyes, the heart of man? It is because God has an exhaustive, crazy kind of love for you. I call it crazy because when you think about it, it cannot be explained!*

> This kind of love is incomprehensible.
> It is breathtaking.
> It is protective, revealing, and chastising.
>
> This kind of love penetrates all barriers;
> the highs and lows that life can bring.
> This kind of love heals wounds more thoroughly
> than any healing that time may bring.

As I think over my past, there are many scenarios that are brought back to my attention. There were circumstances that almost cost me my physical health, and the very sanity that I embrace. As one who specializes in helping others harvest their mental capacity because it is truly the doorway to holistic health, here I stood, the expert, broken, weak, confused, breathless. In the most defenseless state imaginable. Completely depleted and void of any dignity, or self-respect. Wrapped in the swaddling garb of sheer embarrassment, hoping and praying that my deepest and darkest secrets and the flaws in my character would not be exposed for the world to see. Me, the jewel of perfection in the eyes of everyone around me; the saint, the woman of God chosen to lead a remnant for God, has succumbed to some of the same plights that were normal in the everyday life of the atheist and recurrent sinful man. As the tears from the deepest corridors of my being filled the shower floor, mixed in with the filth of my body, my sinful self, the grime and slime of time continued to rewind in my mind. As I fought against myself with such diligence, I was literally in a battle for my soul. I've never fought this hard, never been so exhausted, never felt so alone. But, in the lowest time of my life, in the most detestable state that I could ever be, I heard God whisper to me, "I am here; and if you are ready to win the battle, grab my hand." I prayed to God, "Whatever I need to learn from the lesson and experience, please let me learn quickly; because I can't fight any longer." But, in this moment of helplessness, I found inner strength and determination that I never knew existed. I found myself, I found God. I found freedom. I found solitude and a sanctuary for my heart and the sheer nakedness of me was able to stand and kneel, bare, as God washed over me with His approval. I realized in this moment, that all fear, embarrassment, shame, detest, guilt ... all of it was gone. What I experienced in this moment was the literal removal of every tear from my weary eyes. Though vulnerable with God, I was whole. More sure about everything, not that I can, but God will. I experienced the exhaustive, crazy love of God and now, beginning in this moment, I began to do some radical, crazy, and exhaustive things because I loved God. Sure, in the eyesight of man, they would condemn me. They would scream their legalism and their judgmental rhetoric so intensely that it would slice my soul in two; but I just didn't care. What seemed crazy to man, was actually pleasing and delightful to God. His love, showed me how to love. His devotion and dedication for me at my lowest point showed me how to accept me, flaws and all, unconditionally. So, when I say God's love is exhaustive, crazy, down right insane, it really is, because I experienced it, and now I choose to love the same way. Here, now, ten years later, I am a new woman because I was blessed to encounter God's crazy and exhaustive love for me.

Carl Pinnock penned these words about God's love:

"God's love overflows itself and makes room for creation. Being love, God seeks to share being and communicate presence with it. God is pure ecstasy." [102]

Isn't it interesting that despite God having foreknowledge of all of our sins and transgressions, He still, desired to use His optimum creative design to fashion us for His joy. God creates out of His own abundant interpersonal love; no other reason. There is no hidden agenda or motive for God's design and desire for you. Everything that was placed inside of you, the seed implanted, crying for attentive nurturing, so that it can birth and awaken, is there for your pleasure and God's. This seed, this purpose, is there so that you can mature into love. Abandon the thoughts of control and fairness, as neither of these exist in God's artistry toolkit. You … You were made simply to be loved and to love.

This means then when the enemy attempts to whisper into your ear, all of the inadequacies that you bear. When you have a spiritual replay of all of the historical mistakes, which, with 20/20 vision and a perception change are viewed as the greatest of life's teachable moments; when the enemy tries to use mortal man to hinder your walk and your progress, shift your attention to God's restorative love. God is bound to us by holy choice. Isn't that amazing. That there is nothing more than His choice that leads to His love. This means, then, that there isn't an event, past, present, nor future, that can sever His purposed love for you. This idea of love, as some call it, is thoroughly supported by many love scriptures within the Bible; especially those as in John 3:16 (KJV), that states, "God so loved the world that He gave His only begotten son, that whosoever believeth in Him will not perish but have everlasting life."[103] In this verse, we not only have a profession of God's love, but we also have the action that supports His profession of love towards us. God is closer and more intimate to us than we allow ourselves to believe. God is so preoccupied with man, that He gives Himself away to us, freely, and repetitively. As we think about God's ultimate show of love, we can't help but recognize that there is no greater love. Who among us would lay down their life for another? Some parents may respond and say, "I would lay down my life for my children;" and some children may say, "I will lay down my life for my parents." Even still, some spouses may agree that they would lay down their lives for one another. This may be the case, but what about a wayward spouse or a wayward child who has repeatedly erred and trespassed against you? Would you still sacrifice your life that they may live? What about a child who refused to acknowledge you as their parent and did all manner of evil against you; would you lay down your life for that child? The honest answer is, while there may be one, that one stands alone amongst the millions of others who would yet refuse. But, God's love surpassed our emotional proclivities and defines love in a way that speaks to how we should love "in that while we were yet sinners, Christ died for us." [104]Christ gave His life that you and I might not only have life, but that we might live an abundant life. He died to not only save us, but to redeem and justify us that we might have an opportunity at immortality; reigning with Him in the highest heavens forever. Crazy and exhaustive love is what Christ demonstrated when he left His heavenly abode to walk upon man in a sinful world. Crazy, exhaustive love allowed Him to be born in the lowliest of births; born in a stable and wrapped in milk cloths. Crazy and exhaustive love caused Him to taint His character as a religious leader because He was more concerned about saving the sinful, healing the lepers, and redeeming adulterous women. It was this crazy and exhaustive love that allowed Him to go places and sup with people who were the least among us. Yes, it was crazy, exhaustive love that caused Him to endure slander, lashings, spitting, torture, and subsequently, death on a cross. Why? Why did He endure all of this, when it was within His very power to make heaven and earth stand still? It was all because of His crazy, exhaustive love for you, and the depth of His love, we will never understand. It doesn't make sense … .in this world! While we may never repay, we can pledge everyday to adore God with a response of adoration that mimics as closely as possible, that crazy and exhaustive love for, and to ,Him.

Then, there is this issue of predestination and creation. Predestination is God taking the time and the energy to conceptualize you prior to your manifestation in the earth realm. Let us look at some scriptures to support God's love in the act of predestination.

Ephesians 1: 4-5 : "Even as He chose us in Him before the foundation of the world, that we should be holy and blameless before Him. In love, He predestined us for adoption as sons through Jesus Christ according to the purpose of His will."

Romans 8: 28-30: "And we know that for those who love God all things work together for good, for those who are called according to His purpose. For those whom He foreknew he also predestined to be conformed into the image of HIs son, in order that He might be the firstborn among many brothers. And whose who he predestined, he also called, and those He called, He also justified, and those whom He justified He also glorified."

John 15:16 : "You did not choose me, but I chose you and appointed you that you should go and bear fruit and that your fruit should abide, so that whatever you ask the Father in my name, He may give it to you."

2 Timothy 1:9: "Who saved us and called us to a holy calling, not because of our works, but because of His own purpose and grace which He gave us in Christ Jesus before the ages began.

John 6:44: "No one can come to me unless the Father who sent me draws him. And I will raise him up on the last day."

Ephesians 1: 11-12: "In Him, we have obtained an inheritance. Having been predestined according to the purpose of Him who works all things according to the counsel of His will, so that we who were the first to hope in Christ might be to the praise of His glory."

Galatians 1:15: "But when he who had be set apart before I was born, and who called me by His grace."

Jeremiah 1:5: "Before I shaped you in the womb, I knew all about you. Before you saw the light of day, I had holy plans for you."[105]

Predestination and creation is another example and demonstration of God's unconditional love for us. Many often posit that God only loves us when we do good things, and when we are obedient to Him. I, however, disagree with this concept, as when you consider predestination and creation by the hands of an omnipotent God, why would He even create humanity or individuals knowing all of the sin-filled evils that we would become involved in? Why would God create, knowing the defamation, disrespect, and disappointment He would endure due to our disobedience and glorification of self? You see, the concept of predestination proved that God created us out of His love and filled us with a purpose, according to His plan, before the essence of us was formed. Though we often transgress, this does not prompt God to renege on His love and promises toward us, and it does not prompt God to repossess the gift that is supplanted on the inside of us. God patiently, from a place of unconditional love, awaits the human choice to seek Him; and once this choice is made, God comes in like the nurturing parent, full of compassion and mercy. This compassion and mercy is so great, that Jesus gave His life so that we would have access to the recompense of the Father. Pinnock[106] notes that within God, the movement of self-expression is necessary, but creation is voluntary. But, God's expressing himself in creation is also voluntary, and the fact that God expresses himself in creation and chooses to share His love by creating, is demonstrative of His love for us even before we were born. The decision to create is love! Jesus is strongly correlated and linked to the decision to create again. It is in Jesus that we have new life. After the failure of the immortal, angelic being, and the battle between the creator and the created, the love of Jesus prompted a decision to create again. In our failure, Jesus interceded for humanity because He thought humanity was worth saving and fighting for. Jesus interceded for us because He sees us in light of community and relationship. In fact, Pinnock[107] notes that "the Son gives much focus and attention to the creation because humans are destined for community, mutuality, and relationships. The image of God is really seen in Christ, together with his brothers and sisters; which are you and I." God freely willed creation and freely offers the gift of love to all. This can be seen by all that was created so that you and I can survive; this entire earth and the fullness thereof, is a love offering from God to each of us.

> *2 Peter 3:9: "The Lord is not slow to fulfill His promise as some count slowness, but is patient toward you, not wishing that any should perish, but that all should reach repentance."*

> *1 Peter 1:20 : "He was foreknown before the foundation of the world but was made manifest in the last times for the sake of you."*[108]

Love Gives God the BEST

Reference scripture: Genesis 4 verse 1 -9

LOVE IS A verb and requires action. We demonstrate our love to God by giving Him the BEST of us. It is never too late for new beginnings; pressing forward in the intentional transformation of our minds, our hearts, our motives, focused on giving God our best. The time of perspective change, seeing from a God's eye view and not from our tainted perception, is now. We must forsake the excuses and intentionally press, walking a new step, a Godly step, focused on living a life of peace and prosperity. As we not only plan and prepare to be our BEST, we should spend more time and commit to more resolutions that focus on Giving God our BEST.

Here we revisit the book of Genesis. In establishing the context, we find that after God has made heaven, earth, and all creation, declaring them good. This means God gave us HIS best, creating man and woman in the image of the BEST, and placing in the lush Garden of Eden, which was the BEST environment. We find our first parents defied the rule of law given in the garden of Eden, they allowed Satan's lies to taint their vision and perception, and they began to lust after everything other than God. So, instead of giving God their best, Adam and Eve failed the test and now find themselves outside the garden, and beginning a new life in which they had to till the ground, and work by the sweat of their brow for survival. Even though they were not in the garden, and even though they were disobedient, we find, as we walk into Chapter 4, God's provision still covering them as Adam and Eve conceived their two children, Cain and Abel.

Despite our errors, God continues to give us His best.

IN VERSE ONE, we find Eve declaring that with the help of the Lord, she conceived a man; and in verse 2, she later conceived another: his brother. Both grew, and both were different. Abel was a shepherd, and Cain tilled the ground (farmer).

When it was the time for the offering (harvest), is when the storyline begins to change. It alters a bit; and we see God's examination of the offering, but more importantly, the heart and motives of both Cain and Abel as they make their sacrificial offerings to the Lord. Giving our best must entail giving something precious. Giving God our best is attached to the motives of our heart. I want to pause here for a second, because there is a powerful message in these two verses (3 & 4). From appearances, as we read this passage of scripture, there is no reference as to why God took more delight in the offering of Abel than Cain. Perhaps, then, we can allude to the fact that there was something about the offerings that was different, that is beyond what the naked eye can see.

Cain presented an offering of fruit to the Lord, while Abel also brought a gift-the BEST of the first born from his flock. It says the Lord accepted Abel's offering; but Cain's He did not. We know that a period of time has passed between the extradition from the garden and the events of this chapter. One thing that we know about sacrifices, is that only blood can atone for the sins of man. One, then, can conclude that Cain and Abel, just as the other forefathers of old, were given the directive on what offerings were pleasing and acceptable to the Lord. Cain and Abel, then, were instructed that a sinful man can only approach the Holy God on the grounds of the blood substitutionary sacrifice. However, God also accepts grain offerings. Knowing this, we can better examine and understand, the following verses, and why God was not pleased with Cain's offering.

Cain rejected God's precepts and brought God a bloodless offering. He brought God what was not acceptable. Hebrews 11:4 tells us that, 'By faith, Abel brought God a better offering than Cain.

By faith, he was commended as righteous, when God spoke well of his offering. And by faith, Abel still speaks, even though he is dead! Despite the sacrifice being bloodless, God does accept grain offerings, so there is more to this than the offering; it's the condition of Cain's heart. One can conclude that while Abel brought his best, Cain did not.

Let's look at some possible reasons for Cain's disobedience:

-Pride
-Self Worship
-Lack of Preparation
-Laziness
-Too busy doing what he wanted to do
-Lack of Faith
-Entitlement Issues (1st Born)
-Not listening
-Busyness

Maybe Cain didn't have a relationship with God. Maybe He took God for granted, and because God had always been faithful, and he was so familiar with God, that he felt God would take and bless his mediocrity.

There is a difference between familiarity and relationship!

I question Cain's motive for the unpleasing sacrifice to God. But …

Abel came to the Lord with an offering that was pleasing because His motives were pure, his intentions were just, and he was obedient to the Lord. Abel gave of HIS BEST to the Lord. Scripture was specific about Abel's offering as Abel gave the firstborn of his flock and of their fat. This took time and preparation. I can imagine Abel raising this animal, feeding it extra food, grooming it, maintaining its purity, and raising it with love because He knew he was going to give this gift to the Lord.

Cain, in his disobedience, defied the regulations established by God, but instead of God's rejection prompting a spirit of conviction and repentance, instead of Cain asking God for forgiveness, Cain became filled with anger and disdain for his brother. We find in the story of Cain and Abel, that this entire perplexing sequence of events began due to a spirit of defiance, rebellion, and DISOBEDIENCE. We find both brothers, knowing God's expectations, and what God has ordained, coming before him, presenting an offering to God.

We find one brother, whose heart delighted in God, who was obedient to God, and who was faithful, operating in a spirit of OBEDIENCE, desiring to give his BEST to God; and his sacrifice was accepted.

But, we find a brother, with the "my way or the highway" attitude, bringing "something" to the Lord; and I say, "something," because if the offering is NOT acceptable to God, then, it really is not an offering ... it is "something." Not only did Cain approach God with "something," which was some of his crops, he brought something else-an arrogant and disobedient heart and attitude. While Cain, and many others, may have thought his grains being offered to the Lord was generous, and even noble, God was NOT PLEASED; and he told Cain so. Cain did not give God is BEST.

It is because Cain was disobedient, that the sin continued to grow, leading him down a path of sinful acts that became larger, darker, and ultimately lethal.

So I want to challenge you to GIVE GOD YOUR BEST EVERYDAY!

Why? Because first, there are scripture references all throughout the holy scriptures that admonish us to be obedient, to remain obedient, to walk in obedience, to practice obedience, and to do all to the glory of God.

> -God says if you love me, you will keep my commandments (John 14:15).
> -Blessed are those who hear the word of God and obey it (Luke 11:28).
> -Walk in obedience to all the Lord your God has commanded you, so that you may live and prosper, and prolong your days in the land that you will possess (Deuteronomy 5:33).
> -Do not merely listen to the word, and so deceive yourself; do what it says (James 1:22)!

Crazy love for God desires to give God the best.

We can glean from the very voice of God today. God's loving warning to Cain, and to us, is you will be accepted, if you do what is right and give God your best. We must engage in holistic examination-spirit, soul, and body-which, also, results in examination of our motives. Holistic examination begins with God; we cannot do it ourselves. We must be willing to:

i. LISTEN
ii. ASK
iii. SEE

Listen. Prior to doing the wrong thing, God's instructive voice, as with Cain, whispers in our ear a message of warning or correction. It is at this time that we have to allow our stubborn hearts to become soft and harken to the voice of warning and correction in our ears. The ability to listen is the first step of holistic examination.

Ask. Request to God to purify us—spirit, soul, and body. The spirit is a part of our tri-fold nature that relates to God. It houses our intuition, conscience, and communion with God—our God consciousness. The spirit must be purified. The soul is the part of our tri-fold nature that relates to others and houses our mind, will, and emotions—our self consciousness. The soul must be purified. The body relates to our environment—our world consciousness. It too, must be purified.

We must ask God to purify every aspect of who we are so that our motives and intentions are pure! Ask God to uncover areas in your life where you can practice more obedience. Ask God to show you the secret and hidden errors of your heart. Why? So that you can repent of them, and God can come in with his transforming power and not allow the sin crouching at your door to overtake you.

Lastly, let's discuss seeing. We must possess the ability to see from a godly perspective. When you have been hurt or offended, the jealousy and rage can overtake you and blind you. Ask God to purge your spirit! If you are innocent, you must allow God to vindicate you. You must trust that God will fight for you. God will make your enemies your footstool, and He will protect and shield you from the devices of the enemy. There are many things we cannot see without God's revelatory power. We must ask God to allow us to see our errors and our need to forgive others, and then, we can move into a state of repentance. Real repentance means taking what God has shown us through our spirit examination, and asking that He forgives us for any wrong actions, intentions, motives, or thoughts we may have/or had.

Real repentance, then, means acknowledging to God that your desire is to represent Him, and to put Him first; and that you will not allow your witness to be tainted by responding to offense with offense, purposing always to do the right thing. Repentance conveys, a intentional turning away from sin and a turning to God because you desire to be purged of sinful thoughts, and actions. Love for God triggers a confessing heart, a heart that is heartily sorrowful. This heart will desire to be forgiven from sin; trusting that with the help of God, we will be delivered from repetitious sin.

Purpose to give God your BEST. He thought you were worth creating. He thought you were worth preserving. He thought you were worth SAVING.

Crazy Love for Christ, results in a new you.

I AM: The New is Here!

"Therefore if any man be in Christ, he is a new creature: old things are passed away; behold, all things are become new (2 Corinthians 5:17)."

If I asked you to introduce yourself to someone, what would you say? Would you refer to the roles that you fill? *Hi, I'm a wife, or a mom, or I work for so and so.* Would you mention the things you are passionate about or what you've accomplished; your dream to start a business or enroll in school? Or would you refer to your temperament, describing yourself as strong, disciplined, dependable or shy? It's interesting that we define ourselves by what we do and how we live; whereas God defines us by what He has done. Imagine for a moment, if you shifted your focus from an identity defined by your behavior and began to define your life in light of your God given worth as His child! What would it sound like for you to describe yourself the way God describes you.

Christians are brand-new people on the inside. They have met Jesus! They have professed and formed a relationship with Jesus, God the Father, and the Holy Spirit. The Holy Spirit dwells in us, and gives us new life; and therefore, we are no longer the same. This transformation process is more than a reformation, it is more than a rehabilitation, it is more than a re-education; this transformative process is a re-creation.

Paul, in this letter to the Corinthians, is stating that we are no longer the creation or the creatures we were, prior to developing a union with Christ. This is more than merely turning over a new leaf; it's more than a New Years resolution. This is new life under a new master-our Lord and Savior Jesus the Christ. We are not only changed from within, but a whole new order of creative energy begins with just a touch from Christ. There is a new covenant, a new perspective, a new body, a new church. This is not a superficial change or a novelty that will pass, like that of a fad; this is an entirely new life under the authority of Jesus the Christ. This "newness" allows us to experience life through the eyes of Christ; it admonishes us to remain in step with the Spirit.

We must remember this newness of life is not of any human doing. God, himself, is the orchestrator of the new you! God, himself, began the good work in you. Only God can allow people to approach Him. Only God can satisfy His righteous demands. Only God can save. Remember, you were chosen ON PURPOSE; it is not by happenstance that you are a member of God's family. God's sacrificial work on the cross allowed us to be a part of his family, and because of all of this, I can declare loudly and proudly that – I AM!

> I AM the Imago Dei—a light bearer and reflection of God's light.
> I AM the redeemed of the Lord.
> I AM the head and not the tail.
> I AM above and not beneath.
> I AM more than a conqueror through Christ who strengthens me.
> I AM Holy and Righteous through Christ my Savior.
> I AM cleansed from all sin and as white as snow.
> I AM prosperous because God maketh my soul prosper.
> I AM a temple of the Holy Spirit.
> I AM a chosen generation, a Royal Priesthood, a Holy Nation.

I AM peculiar. Odd. Different— whatever you want to call it.

I AM His workmanship; created in Him unto good works.

I AM ordained.

I AM a branch connected to the vine of life.

I Bear much fruit.

I AM a friend of God; He calls me friend.

I AM like Christ.

I AM a child of God.

I AM loved.

I AM born of God and the evil one cannot touch me.

I AM the salt of the earth.

I AM the light of the world.

I AM a joint heir with Christ.

I AM established, anointed, and sealed by God in Christ; given to the Holy Spirit as a pledge, guaranteeing my inheritance to come.

I AM a new creation.

I AM more than a conqueror through Christ who strengthens me.

I AM the one chosen in Christ before the foundation of the world to be holy and without blame before Him.

I AM a citizen of heaven with a mansion and direct access to my God.

I don't know about you, but, I recognize that I AM fearfully and wonderfully made.

I AM a creation, an image bearer of the great I AM, who was, who IS, and who is yet to come.

Jesus saw, He came, He walked, He talked, He sacrificed and He saved!

So, with the power, position, and prestige that He has given to me as a member of the household of faith, I declare the new me is here!

God sacrificed so much for you to understand and realize who you are, and to not walk according any of the "I can't" or "I'm not" statements. We must walk intentionally, knowing for sure that I AM! God sacrificed His life so that you can stand firm and declare "I AM a son/daughter of the great I AM." Step into your Christ centered identity wear new labels doused in spiritually sound truths. Your identity is found in knowing who you are as His child and believing that belonging to Him matters most of all. Take off the old you, and boldly declare — I AM! The new me is HERE!

1. Reaffirm your position in Christ. Pray and ask God for restoration
2. Take your place as a child of God.
3. Walk in the new life given to you by God.

Crazy, exhaustive love for Christ.

Epilogue

Our goal in this life it to become pre-destination manifestation. Our becoming demonstrates to the world, and more specifically our enemy, that we as God's creation delight in worshipping Him in spirit and in truth. The heart centered journey is all about partnering with God. It is during this journey that we become divine tools, partnering with our God, to bring about His divine will, and pledging allegiance to be a part of His family and subject to His rule, forever. While this life is full of deceptions, false truths, and fake realities, we as believers can rest assured that we are never without a guide, and we are never without protection and provision. I know there are times where it feels like you are wandering in the dark, but I am here to turn on the light. The first step in being found, is acknowledging that you are in the dark; that you are lost! By reading this work, it is my prayer that you have not only found the light of our loving God, but that you have rested in

His finished work concerning you. You were created with intention, purpose, and a crazy exhaustive love. Walk authentically, following the guidance of the Holy Spirit, in the footsteps of Christ, toward the heavenly above of God our Father.

Biography

Rev. Sha'Leda Mirra, was born April 25, 1982 in Lake City Fl. Rev. Mirra has shared a God ordained union with Mr. Christopher Mirra for eighteen years and from this union were born two beautiful daughters Cadence (17) and Chrystian (9) Mirra. Rev. Mirra is the proud pastor of Union African Methodist Episcopal Church in Lake City Fl, where she and her family have served since November of 2018. Rev. Mirra accepted her call into the ministry in 2011, and has since this time devoted her life to leading others to the Way. She is the owner and therapist of a successful private practice in Lake City Florida known as The Heart Centered Journey, Counseling, Coaching, & Consultation. In addition to her private practice, Rev. Mirra is also a faculty member at Saint Leo University teaching Undergraduate Social Work and is also the founder and president of a non-profit agency Daughters of Eve, Inc. which focuses on holistic wellness for African American women. As a life-long resident in Columbia County, Mrs. Mirra has served as a community activist, advocating for causes such as child abuse and neglect, domestic violence, and mental health education within the African American community. In addition, much focus has been devoted to consulting within the spiritual community to improve education and equip the spiritual community with essential resources to resume their role as the help seeking entity within the community.

Rev. Mirra is a graduate of Saint Leo University, receiving two master's degrees in both Criminology and Social Work. Presently, Mrs. Mirra is actively pursuing her PhD in Psychology with Capella University, and just completed her master's degree in Divinity from Regent University. Rev. Mirra has a passion for ministry and education, as both are an integral part of impacting the lives of others within the community. Rev. Mirra lives by the motto: "everywhere you go, remember who you represent", and purposes to live a life of faithfulness and dedication to our Lord Jesus Christ.

Connect With
SHA'LEDA MIRRA
ON SOCIAL MEDIA

Facebook.......................... @heartcenteredjourney
Instagram .... @heartcenteredjourney
Twitter .... @mirrasha

WEBSITE
www.theheartcenteredjourneycccinc.com

Endnotes

1. Holy Bible. English Standard Version (2011), Crossway.
2. ESV
3. Symptom. 2019. In *Merriam-Webster.com*. Retrieved April 1, 2019 from https://www.meriam-webster.com/dictionary/symptom.
4. Jalāl al-Dīn Rūmī., & Barks, C. (1996). *The essential Rumi*. 1st HarperCollins paperback ed. San Francisco, CA: Harper.
5. *The Holy Bible, new international version, (1984)*. Grand Rapids: Zondervan Publishing House.
6. *The Holy Bible, new international version, (1984)*. Grand Rapids: Zondervan Publishing House.
7. *The Holy Bible, new international version, (1984)*. Grand Rapids: Zondervan Publishing House.
8. *The Holy Bible, new international version, (1984)*. Grand Rapids: Zondervan Publishing House.
9. Bella Grace Magazine.
10. Jalāl, -D. R., & Barks, C. (2002). *The soul of Rumi: A new collection of ecstatic poems*. New York: HarperCollins.

11. *The Holy Bible, new international version, (1984).* Grand Rapids: Zondervan Publishing House.

12. "Montage." *Dictionary*. 2019. Retrieved December 2019 from: https://www.dictionary.com.

13. Simmons, Ruth (2017). *Graceland.* Oregon: Harvest House.

14. Pinnock, C. (1999). *The flame of love: A theology of the Holy Spirit.* Downers Grove, Ill: InterVarstiy Press.

15. Atticus. (2017). Love Her Wild. Atticus Poetry.

16. *The Holy Bible, new international version, (1984).* Grand Rapids: Zondervan Publishing House.

17. Merton, Thomas (1961). *New Seeds of Contemplation.* New York: New Directions Publishing.

18. Smith, James K.A. (2016). *You are what you love.* Grand Rapids: Baker Publishing Group.

19. Scazzero, P. (2017). *Emotionally healthy spirituality.* Grand Rapids, MI: Zondervan.

20. *The Holy Bible, new international version, (1984).* Grand Rapids: Zondervan Publishing House.

21. *The Holy Bible, new international version, (1984).* Grand Rapids: Zondervan Publishing House.

22. *The Holy Bible, new international version, (1984).* Grand Rapids: Zondervan Publishing House

23. *The Holy Bible, new international version, (1984).* Grand Rapids: Zondervan Publishing House

24. *The Holy Bible, new international version, (1984).* Grand Rapids: Zondervan Publishing House

25. *The Holy Bible, new international version, (1984).* Grand Rapids: Zondervan Publishing House

26 *The Holy Bible, new international version, (1984)*. Grand Rapids: Zondervan Publishing House

27 *The Holy Bible, new international version, (1984)*. Grand Rapids: Zondervan Publishing House

28 Bevere, J. (2014). *The bait of Satan*. Lake Mary, FL: Charisma House.

29 *The Holy Bible, new international version, (1984)*. Grand Rapids: Zondervan Publishing House

30 *The Holy Bible, new international version, (1984)*. Grand Rapids: Zondervan Publishing House

31 *The Holy Bible, new international version, (1984)*. Grand Rapids: Zondervan Publishing House

32 Loehr, J. (2007). *The power of story*. New York, NY: Simon & Schuster, Inc.

33 *The Holy Bible, new international version, (1984)*. Grand Rapids: Zondervan Publishing House

34 *The Holy Bible, new international version, (1984)*. Grand Rapids: Zondervan Publishing House

35 *The Holy Bible, new international version, (1984)*. Grand Rapids: Zondervan Publishing House

36 Wilkinson, B. (2009). *You were born for this*. Colorado Springs, CO: Multnomah Books.

37 *The Holy Bible, new international version, (1984)*. Grand Rapids: Zondervan Publishing House

38 ESV

39 ESV

40 ESV

41 *The Holy Bible, new international version, (1984)*. Grand Rapids: Zondervan Publishing House

42 Choice. 2019. In Merriam-Webster.com. Retrieved May 8, 2019, from https://www.merriam-webster.com/dictionary/choice.

43 *The Holy Bible, new international version, (1984).* Grand Rapids: Zondervan Publishing House

44 *The Holy Bible: New Testament: ESV English Standard Version.* (2009). Wheaton, IL: Crossway.

45 *The Holy Bible: New Testament: ESV English Standard Version.* (2009). Wheaton, IL: Crossway.

46 ESV

47 *The Holy Bible, new international version, (1984).* Grand Rapids: Zondervan Publishing House

48 ESV

49 Augustine. (1996). *The confessions of Saint Augustine.* Springdale, PA: Whitaker House.

50 Scazzero, P. (2017). *Emotionally healthy spirituality.* Grand Rapids, MI: Zondervan.

51 Jalāl al-Dīn Rūmī., & Barks, C. (1996). *The essential Rumi.* 1st HarperCollins paperback ed. San Francisco, CA: Harper

52 *The Holy Bible, new international version, (1984).* Grand Rapids: Zondervan Publishing House.

53 Jalāl al-Dīn Rūmī., & Barks, C. (1996). *The essential Rumi.* 1st HarperCollins paperback ed. San Francisco, CA: Harper

54 *The Holy Bible, new international version, (1984).* Grand Rapids: Zondervan Publishing House.

55 ESV

56 ESV

57 *The Holy Bible, new international version, (1984).* Grand Rapids: Zondervan Publishing House.

58 *The Holy Bible, new international version, (1984).* Grand Rapids: Zondervan Publishing House.

59 *The Holy Bible, new international version, (1984).* Grand Rapids: Zondervan Publishing House

60 Willard, D. (1991). *The spirit of the disciplines.* Sanfrancisco, CA: Harper Collins.

61 *The Holy Bible, new international version, (1984).* Grand Rapids: Zondervan Publishing House

62 *The Holy Bible, new international version, (1984).* Grand Rapids: Zondervan Publishing House

63 *The Holy Bible, new international version, (1984).* Grand Rapids: Zondervan Publishing House

64 *The Holy Bible, new international version, (1984).* Grand Rapids: Zondervan Publishing House

65 *The Holy Bible, new international version, (1984).* Grand Rapids: Zondervan Publishing House

66 "Intentional." *Dictionary.* 2019. Retrieved December 2019 from: https://www.dictionary.com.

67 Drucker, Peter.

68 *The Holy Bible, new international version, (1984).* Grand Rapids: Zondervan Publishing House.

69 *The Holy Bible: New Testament: ESV English Standard Version.* (2009). Wheaton, IL: Crossway

70 *The Holy Bible: New Testament: ESV English Standard Version.* (2009). Wheaton, IL:Crossway

71 Trimm, C. (2011). *The 40 day soul fast.* Destiny Image.

72 Jones, K. (2007). *Holy play: The joyful adventure of unleashing your divine purpose.* San Francisco, CA: Jossey-Bass.

73 *The Holy Bible, new international version, (1984).* Grand Rapids: Zondervan Publishing House.

74 Trimm, C. (2017). Conference Speech.

75 *The Holy Bible: New Testament: ESV English Standard Version.* (2009). Wheaton, IL: Crossway.

76 *The Holy Bible: New Testament: ESV English Standard Version.* (2009). Wheaton, IL: Crossway.

77 *The Holy Bible: New Testament: ESV English Standard Version.* (2009). Wheaton, IL: Crossway.

78 *The Holy Bible: New Testament: New English Translation.* (2005). Biblical Studies Press.

79 "Bitter." *Dictionary.* 2019. Retrieved December 2019 from:https://www.dictionary.com.

80 *The Holy Bible, new international version, (1984).* Grand Rapids: Zondervan Publishing House.

81 Brand, C., Draper, C., & England, A. (2003). *Holman Illustrated Bible Dictionary.* Nashville, TN: Holman Bible Publishers.

82 *The Holy Bible, new international version, (1984).* Grand Rapids: Zondervan Publishing House.

83 *The Holy Bible, new international version, (1984).* Grand Rapids: Zondervan Publishing House.

84 ESV

85 *The Holy Bible, new international version, (1984).* Grand Rapids: Zondervan Publishing House.

86 *The Holy Bible, new king james version, (2010).* Nashville, TN: Thomas Nelson Publishers.

87 *The Holy Bible, new king james version, (2010).* Nashville, TN: Thomas Nelson Publishers.

88   Cowman, L.B. (2016). *Streams in the desert morning and evening 365 devotions.* Grand Rapids, MI: Zondervan.

89   *The Holy Bible, new king james version, (2010).* Nashville, TN: Thomas Nelson Publishers.

90   *The Holy Bible, new king james version, (2010).* Nashville, TN: Thomas Nelson Publishers.

91   *The Holy Bible, new king james version, (2010).* Nashville, TN: Thomas Nelson Publishers.

92   Wilkinson, B. (2009). *You were born for this.* Colorado Springs, CO: Multnomah Books.

93   *The Holy Bible, new king james version, (2010).* Nashville, TN: Thomas Nelson Publishers.

94   Strong, A.H. Quote.

95   *The Holy Bible, new international version, (1984).* Grand Rapids: Zondervan Publishing House.

96   *The Holy Bible, new international version, (1984).* Grand Rapids: Zondervan Publishing House.

97   Eckhardt, J. (2017). *The prophets manual.* Lake Mary, FL: Charisma House.

98   Willard, D. (1991). *The spirit of the disciplines.* San Francisco, CA: Harper Collins.

99   *The Holy Bible, new international version, (1984).* Grand Rapids: Zondervan Publishing House.

100 *The Holy Bible, new king james version, (2010).* Nashville, TN: Thomas Nelson Publishers.

101 *The Holy Bible, new king james version, (2010).* Nashville, TN: Thomas Nelson Publishers.

102 Pinnock, C. (1999). *The flame of love: A theology of the Holy Spirit.* Downers Grove, Ill: InterVarstiy Press.

103 *The Holy Bible, new king james version, (2010).* Nashville, TN: Thomas Nelson Publishers.

104 Romans 5:8 NIV

105 *The Holy Bible, new king james version, (2010).* Nashville, TN: Thomas Nelson Publishers.

106 Pinnock, C. (1999). *The flame of love: A theology of the Holy Spirit.* Downers Grove, Ill: InterVarstiy Press.

107 Pinnock, C. (1999). *The flame of love: A theology of the Holy Spirit.* Downers Grove, Ill: InterVarstiy Press.

108 *The Holy Bible, new king james version, (2010).* Nashville, TN: Thomas Nelson Publishers.

www.ingramcontent.com/pod-product-compliance
Lightning Source LLC
Chambersburg PA
CBHW052024070526
44584CB00016B/1888